17.95

DATE DUE		
APR 29 1994		
May 27		
NOV 22 1994		
DEC 1 8 1997		
APR 2 4 1998		
AUG 1 1 1998		
APR 9 - 2000		
DEC 1 9 2000		
JUL 2 3 2006		

Venturing

An Introduction
to Sailing

Venturing

An Introduction to Sailing

by Peter Burchard
with photographs
by the author

Little, Brown and Company
Boston/Toronto

First Edition

Library of Congress Cataloging-in-Publication Data

Burchard, Peter.
    Venturing: an introduction to sailing.
    Bibliography: p.
    Includes index.
    1. Sailing—Juvenile literature.   2. Seamanship—
Juvenile literature.   I. Title.
GV811.B83 1986   797.1'24   85-24032
ISBN 0-316-11613-0

*Unless otherwise noted, all photographs in this book were taken
by the author.*
                         HC
*Published simultaneously in Canada
by Little, Brown & Company (Canada) Limited*

Printed in the United States of America

For Malcolm Nicholls

Contents

Part 1

Looking Forward

Part 2

Sailing

Part 3

Learning the Ropes

Acknowledgments

Thanks to my many sailing friends — catboat sailor Rosalind McCagg; racing skipper Danny Miller; senior yachtsman John Streeter; Revell Carr, director of the Mystic Seaport Museum; Rob Pittaway, naval architect and small-boat designer; sailmakers Peter Conrad and Kevin Farrar; Bill Dunbar, president of the International Blue Jay Class Association; Betsy O'Brien, Johnathan Farrar, Carter Gowrie, James McCullough, and Bill Nicholls. Thanks to Sparkman and Stephens, the designers of the Blue Jay and of many grand prix yachts. Last but by no means least, thanks to Robby Robinson of *Sail* magazine for his help in making this a better book than it might otherwise have been.

P.B.

Venturing

An Introduction
to Sailing

Part 1

Looking Forward

First Steps

I learned to sail on a small New Hampshire lake, in an awkward little boat — flat-bottomed with a single sail and a flimsy centerboard. The waters of the lake were warm. On good days, there was very little danger and I learned by trial and error. Someone told me to let out the sail when the wind was behind me and to pull it in when I was going more or less against the wind. They said I would have to zigzag as I made my way upwind. The boom whacked me several times, but it was small and I survived. I don't recommend this method. I advise you to begin with a sound boat and a competent instructor.

Throughout the world, there are programs that provide fleets of boats and instructors in the basic sailing skills. Most yacht clubs have sailing programs for beginners. Many people who belong to yacht clubs buy their own boats, but most yacht clubs, even small ones, have a few boats they can lend. There are many sailing schools and sailing camps. Town and city governments have sailing schools in public parks. Most sailing programs provide good teachers, who relate beginning skills to future needs, as ocean racing skipper Ted Jones did when he wrote, "To sail slowly or inefficiently is to be unseamanlike. The sea demands efficiency, and to be timid or indecisive is to invite disaster."

As you learn, a range of possibilities will appear. Alone, or with a friend, in fair weather, you may sail close to home, exploring islands and inlets. You may race your own small boat or sail as crew aboard an ocean racing boat, braving storms and heavy seas. Someday, you may make long voyages, as did the greatest mariners

Docking at a sailing school in the Charles River Basin, Boston.

from the Norsemen to today's bravest and most skillful sailors.

Wind and Water

Before you venture out to sail, you can learn many things just by looking at the water and by reading about tides and currents.

Waves wash the shores of oceans, lakes, and ponds. Imagine you are standing on the *lee* shore of a bay — standing in a place toward which the wind is blowing. As you look across the bay, you can see the effect of wind on water, not just in the larger waves. A gust of wind is visible, coming toward you. Though you cannot see the air, you can watch wind streak the water, feel it as it strikes your face, see it as it pushes waves that curl and shatter on the sand.

On an ocean beach, waves are often very large, as they are on the beaches of Hawaii. In what is called the roaring forties — the southern latitudes in which the wind romps largely unobstructed all the way around the earth — waves grow very large indeed. Sometimes they reach enormous heights and play with ships as if the ships were bathtub toys.

Patterns that wind makes on water are a clue to its force and direction. For me, in daylight, such patterns are the most reliable of indicators. When the wind shifts, large waves are slow to change, but the shift is imme-

Look for catspaws on the water.

diately written in the *catspaws* — little ridges on the water. Catspaws have a parabolic shape, something like a boomerang. These indicate true wind.

What's the difference betweeen true wind and apparent wind? If you stand on a flat plain holding high a light windsock, the windsock indicates true wind. If you run, let's say, at right angles to the wind, the windsock indicates apparent wind. In other words, apparent wind is a mixture of true wind and the wind that is created by your forward motion.

As you study the effect of wind on water, you will learn to read the catspaws. When you sail, as you venture into currents — river currents, tidal currents, ocean currents —there will be times when catspaws disappear completely. Currents and important wind shifts change

the language of the water. For example, in a river when the water flows downstream and the wind is blowing upstream, there may be great turbulence on the surface of the water, as if schools of very large fish are in constant combat there. At times like these, you will need to use other indicators of the wind's direction, things mounted on your boat, *telltales* or a *masthead fly* — bits of yarn or strips of plastic on the sails, or a kind of weathervane atop the mast.

One day, you may sail aboard a boat equipped with an A.P.I. — an apparent wind indicator. This is no more than a gauge that tells the helmsman where the masthead fly is pointing. Even when you use sophisticated instruments, you will still need basic skills, which you acquire as you begin to learn to sail.

A Small Boat

If you enroll in a sailing program, someone else will have chosen your boat for you. In choosing a boat for this book to describe and photograph, I talked to experts — sailing teachers, cruising sailors, ocean racing skippers, sailmakers, and designers of small boats. Many mentioned the Blue Jay as a boat that would suit my purposes, and maybe yours as well, so this popular small boat appears throughout the pages of this book. Other small boats might have been as good a choice, but the Blue Jay is an almost perfect boat for beginners.

In a sense, the Blue Jay and other well-designed small boats are little sisters of 12-meter boats, built for America's Cup competition. The Blue Jay's *Marconi rig* —

Blue Jays at the starting line.

Winning.

a rig using tall triangular sails — can be handled easily, and when you are ready you can sail her with a little *spinnaker*, a thin balloonlike sail that gives the boat extra speed when you are moving more or less with the wind.

You can find fleets of Blue Jays and other small class-boats in the Northwest, in the South, on the West Coast, in the East, in inland states and Canada, east and west. Bright children ten years old can learn to sail boats like these, yet many adults own and race them.

Learn the Lingo

In this book, you will find diagrams and a glossary of terms. Using these and explanations in the text, you can learn what to call the sections of the boat, the sails, and the parts of the rigging.

First concentrate on things you can reach out and touch as you move around the boat, parts of the hull, the rigging and the sails, the fittings and the gear. Later, as you start to sail, you will learn other words that have to do with such matters as rights of way and points of sailing. Some terms, like *tumblehome* — the inward curve of the topside of a boat — are charming but not essential, and they won't appear in my glossary.

As far as possible, I will define words as I use them. I won't define common terms like *bow* and *stern* in the

This diagram includes parts of the boat and parts of the sail. All of these terms appear in the glossary.

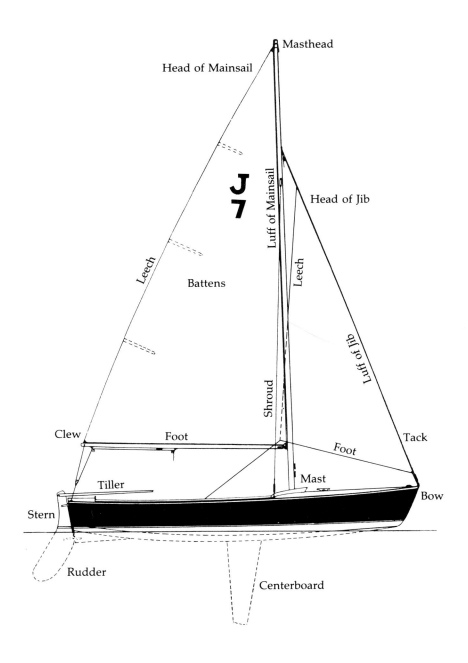

Masthead

Head of Mainsail

Luff of Mainsail

Head of Jib

Leech

Leech

Luff of Jib

Battens

Shroud

Clew

Foot

Foot

Tack

Tiller

Mast

Bow

Stern

Rudder

Centerboard

text, but you will find all special words that refer to boats and sailing listed in the glossary. Many will appear in diagrams and captions, too.

If at first you are impatient with these salty sounding words and wonder why a sailor's language is so different from a landsman's, remember that every sport and every skill has a language of its own. A sailor's language is among the oldest, having roots in ancient times.

Later, when you know the language well, you may want to change the rules, speak a language of your own. Seasoned sailors sometimes laugh at sailing terms. I sailed two years aboard an ocean racing boat. In *Blixtar*, we sometimes called a *deck* a floor. A *bulkhead* became a wall. Instead of *tacking*, we flopped over, but in dangerous circumstances, we were glad to know and use the proper words so there could be no misunderstanding. Because you will sail with someone else and will talk to other sailors, learn the common language of the boat and the sea.

Know the Boat

Board the boat you plan to sail on a calm day or when she is on dry land. Since she will be the instrument in which you will learn the art of sailing, spend a little time with her.

If the rudder is removable, as it is on most small boats, practice putting it in place. Slide it into the *gudgeons* — the fittings on the hull into which the rudder *pintles* are inserted. If you do this several times, you will get the hang of it.

Simple rudder installation, common to almost all centerboarders.

Learn to use the *centerboard*. There will be times when you will want the board down all the way, times when you want it up and other times when you want it in an intermediate position. Right now you can play with it. Drop it. Pull it up, cleating and uncleating what is called the *pendant* or *pennant* — the light line which holds it up.

The *running rigging* is made up of ropes with which you will raise and trim the sails — halyards and sheets. The *standing rigging* consists of wires which hold the mast in place — stays and shrouds.

Assuming that the mast is *stepped* — put in place — and that the standing rigging is in place, you can learn about the running rigging by manipulating it.

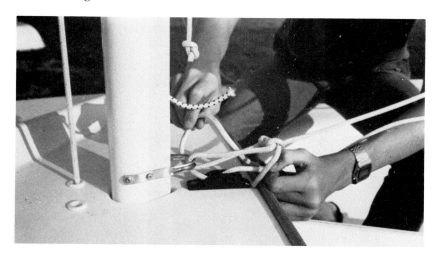

Rigging vang, leading line through a jam cleat.

Stepping the mast. If you have to hoist the mast into place, it's better if you have someone help you.

With *halyards,* you will raise your sails. Halyards are so named because in square-rigged sailing ships the sails are made fast to a *spar,* called a yard. When sailors in the old square riggers raised the sails, they "hauled the yard." This was shortened to halyard. Before you tug at any halyard, make sure the *shackle* at one end is secured to something — to a sail or to the *bale* — a kind of metal loop on the mast. Otherwise, it may rise up to a place beyond your reach. For exactly the same reason, make sure you *cleat* the other end. If you do this right away, you will avoid making what is probably the most common of mistakes — letting go a halyard.

When you have checked all the halyards, play with them. See how they work, which sails they will be at-

Sorting out the halyards.

Line wrapped properly around a cleat. At first, take two round turns, then wrap as shown.

tached to. Most halyards on small boats run outside the mast. Some run inside the mast and are called *internal halyards*. In either case, you will soon see how yours work. Incidentally, if your boat does have internal halyards, make sure you tie a figure-eight knot at the end with no shackle on it so that if by chance you pull the shackle end, you won't lose the other end. When in doubt about the uses of a halyard, move it slightly to make sure which one it is.

Unbag your sails. If possible, spread them out on a lawn or clean flat place. Again consulting diagrams, learn their sections and their parts so when you put them on, you won't fumble.

From boat to boat, the standing rigging varies widely. Standing rigging is designed to take many kinds of stresses. For example, when you sail with the wind,

Detail of a shroud, showing simple installation using a circular cotter pin.

the *backstay* — the wire which runs from the masthead to the stern — will be taut, and when you face the wind, it will be slack. When the wind is coming from the port-side — left side — of your boat, the *shrouds* on the port-side will be taut and the starboard ones — the ones on the right side — will be slack. I tell you this so that when you start to sail, a slack shroud or stay will not alarm you.

Incidentally, most large boats are equipped with an adjustable backstay. Some of these can be tightened using an hydraulic system. Blue Jays have no backstay. In any case, the adjustment of one portion of the standing rigging will affect the rig as a whole and in turn the performance of your boat. Adjusting stays and shrouds, called the *tuning* of the rigging, is a complicated business and it varies from boat to boat, as does the rig. With the

Lines may become tangled like masses of spaghetti, but they can be sorted out in a short time.

help of a teacher, or a sailor who has wide experience, learn how to rig your boat — step the mast and secure the shrouds and stays.

Most rigs are designed so that you can *reef* the mainsail — shorten the amount of sail exposed to the wind. Acquaint yourself with the system on the boat you plan to sail. In general, it is easier to reef before you sail and to shake a reef out when under way.

As you explore your boat, be patient. When you know her fittings and her gear as well as you know your own hands and their capabilities, when you can move with perfect ease around her cockpit and around her deck, you can start to think of sailing.

Mate and Skipper

By now, you have learned a lot of things about the boat you plan to sail, about the water and the wind. Now you want to do some sailing, with a mate. You want to make your own mistakes and learn from them, as well you should.

Armed with knowledge, you can start right away to be a skipper or a mate who is self-assured and fair. You and your mate, whoever he or she may be, will be learning things together and will soon become a team.

A good skipper asks crew members for advice but is always in command. Even on a quiet day, situations can arise that demand quick decisions and skillful moves.

Mate and skipper.

As you learn, don't take passengers along. Sail with people who can help you. No matter how small your boat is, or how quiet the day is, you are responsible for everyone who is on board.

When you have to give commands, give them in a quiet, steady voice, and be firm if necessary. I sailed with ocean racing skipper Danny Miller for two years, in sudden North Atlantic squalls, through gusty starlit nights, in cold weather, and in steamy tropic days. In all the time I sailed with him, I never heard him raise his voice, except to be heard above the wind when it whistled in the rigging. His is a good example. Follow it.

Part 2

Sailing

Wind and Sky

In most places, afternoons are windier than mornings are. In San Francisco Bay at some times of the year, winds are light to moderate in the mornings and by early afternoon are blowing hard, often more than 30 miles per hour. During the New England sailing season, things are less predictable, but in general, quiet mornings herald breezy afternoons. Tidal changes sometimes bring a change in wind.

Try to notice weather patterns in the region where you sail, but don't rely on yourself or on other amateurs. Before you sail, check the weather carefully. You can do this by using a small VHF radio or by talking to someone who has one — a fisherman or the owner of a larger boat. Weather broadcasts sponsored by the National Oceanic and Atmospheric Administration (NOAA) may be heard coast to coast on VHF radios. In a pinch, you can call a Coast Guard station. They will give you a report, but they are often busy, sometimes with urgent business. If you can, depend on your own radio.

Small craft warnings should be heeded by beginning sailors. These are aired on NOAA radio, and yacht clubs and Coast Guard stations signal them by flying a single red triangular flag. Incidentally, two red triangular flags, one flying above the other, signal a gale warning. Few sailors venture out of port in gales. In general, small-boat sailors should stay home if winds are blowing more than 20 miles per hour.

Boarding

Because docking and undocking are maneuvers that require basic sailing skills, I will start by supposing that your boat, or the boat you will be sailing, is kept on a *mooring* — a permanent anchor consisting of a length of chain *shackled* to an *anchor rode,* a rope, which in this case is called a pendant or a pennant, kept afloat by a small buoy of some kind when not in use.

To make things easier, I will assume that your boat is not too near other boats. She is swinging in wind changes but is pointing more or less toward the direction from which the wind is coming. If your boat is at a dock or a launching ramp and you already have begun to learn to sail, turn to page 60, where I explain how to sail away from docks and ramps and how to return to them.

You may row out to your mooring. If you do, use common sense about the *dinghy* — the small rowboat you are using. Step into the middle of it and with your mate distribute weight so you won't capsize it. Row directly upwind — toward the wind — as you come up alongside your sailboat. If you row straight at your sailboat the wind will blow you down on her and you will hit her forcefully. With a *bowline,* tie the *painter* — the rope fastened to the dinghy's bow — to a shroud, or cleat it near your sailboat's stern. As you board the boat, be careful. Step across the narrow deck or rail into the cockpit.

If someone takes you to your boat in a launch, wait until the motorboat loses *way* — forward motion. Then reach out for a handhold on your boat. Be careful not to pinch your hand between the two boats. The first person to board the sailboat should let down the centerboard, pushing it down by hand if necessary. This will increase your boat's stability.

When you decide in which direction you will sail, untie the dinghy from whatever it is tied to and retie it to the pendant. The dinghy with its painter and the pendant must be on the side of the forestay opposite to the direction you'll be sailing in. If you have to lead the dinghy from one side to the other of your boat, hold the painter firmly and lead it around the stern. The dinghy will drift astern naturally, with the wind, whereas it would be difficult to lead it around the bow. Most mooring pendants have a loop at their ends. This loop is probably around the bow cleat or a bow fitting on your boat. With a bowline, tie the painter to this loop, at the same time that you keep the loop around the cleat. The dinghy will remain tied to the loop when you sail.

Both of you should be wearing life vests or life jackets. Vests are less cumbersome, so, if you have a choice, wear life vests. Even a vest may seem a burden when the day is very warm and things are going as they should, but wear one anyway. It takes energy to stay afloat after a dunking, and in an emergency you will need your energy for other things.

Run down your equipment list. Is everything you need on board? Make sure all the things you carry are secure in cloth pouches or tied down. Your anchor, paddles, boat hook, and extra life vests can be stowed out of the way and tied with light, strong line. Use knots you know can easily be untied.

If your boat has full flotation, as it should, and *inspection ports* — large covered holes — make sure the flotation tanks are dry and that the holes are firmly sealed. However little chance there is that your boat leaks, check

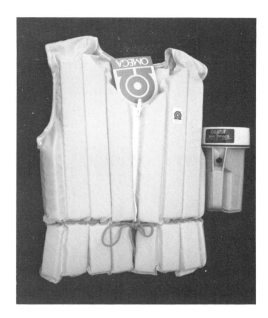

Life vest and a lantern which will float if it falls overboard.

the tanks after storms and long periods of rain. In fact, during rainy spells, you may have to bail your boat from time to time, even if it is equipped with a *boom tent* — a canvas or plastic covering that fits over the boom and is tied to the sides of the boat.

Even short voyages should be planned. Seasoned skippers plan short sails on familiar waters in a minute, maybe less. Go your own pace. Understand what you are doing.

Once, with a friend who had been a foredeck captain in a grand prix racing boat, I planned a sail. In a ship's store, we scanned a *chart* — a kind of nautical road map — shrugged, and turned away. No need to buy the chart. There was one aboard the boat, and we had sailed on Nantucket Sound many times. No problem there. Aboard the boat, I consulted what turned out to be an old chart. Not only was it out of date, but it was worn and taped together. Parts of it were hard to read. We set sail in brisk winds, which grew stronger as we sailed. The condition of our chart, combined with careless planning, put us two miles off the course we should have sailed, and took us into shallow waters where we might have run aground and damaged our small boat. As it was, we were lucky and we found the buoyed channel we were looking for, which led to a sheltered port.

A Quick Look at Chart and Compass

For me, few things are more exciting than unfolding or unrolling charts and planning day sails, overnights, and longer cruises. You may soon feel the same way.

Before you sail, you should buy a detailed chart of the waters you will be sailing in. As you go, figure out more or less where you are in relation to the things around you. Above the treetops, you may see the chimney of the house you've lived in all your life, and the flagpole on the point. Even so, when you sail, spot the buoys, islands, lighthouses, and conspicuous landmarks, as well as their distances from you. If you do this constantly, you will know how to skirt shoals and hazards which are marked on your chart, and where to sail when fog rolls in.

Point your hand-bearing compass north, east, south, and west,* noting landmarks and seamarks. Now, mak-

* Marked N, E, S, W, and/or 0°, 90°, 180°, 270°.

ing sure it is far enough away from metal objects on your boat or in your pockets, move the compass back to north.

On your chart, find this direction. It is indicated on what is called a *compass rose* by an arrow, and the word MAGNETIC. Don't confuse this compass rose with the slightly larger one outside it or the one inside it, if there is one. If you spend a little time with your hand-bearing compass and your chart, you will soon figure out pretty much where you are. If there is a compass mounted on the boat, you will soon see how to use it.

If you can see one or more buoys on the water, find them on your chart. In this book, you will find an illustration of the different kinds of *markers*. Channel markers — buoys marking limits of a channel — are almost always red and green, nuns and cans. *Nuns* are tapered at their tops. *Cans* are squared off at their tops. Both are mostly numbered buoys. Nun number 10 is marked N "10" and can number 10 is marked C "10" and so on. Flashing buoys are equipped with lights that send out signals, some of which are almost invisible in daylight. A buoy that is programmed to flash every four seconds is marked Fl 4sec. Bell buoys are marked BELL. There are many kinds of buoys and as many abbreviations for them. Rocks are marked with a kind of asterisk, like a six-pointed star. These are rocks that under almost all conditions you can see above the surface of the water. The numbers scattered all around your chart, as if at random, indicate depth at low tide. If the bottom of your centerboard or keel is four feet below the surface of the water, that is if you *draw* four feet, you can sail in places marked five feet or deeper at low tide. The abbreviations Rk, Rky, and Rks signify a rock or rocks. Such areas are often marked FOUL.

On this portion of a chart are marked many numbers indicating the depth of water at low tide. There are buoys to follow if you want to enter Little Harbor. In the lower left-hand corner of the chart is a green gong buoy marked with the number 1. Nun number 4, which is red, and tapered at its top, is positioned between a bell that flashes red every four seconds, and a buoy marking Great Ledge — a place to stay away from since it consists of several rocks clustered in a shallow place. If you find these four buoys, you will soon identify other buoys on the chart.

The tower on Nobska Point is 87 feet high, has a horn, a light that flashes every six seconds, and a radio beacon that sends a signal out to ships and boats that have short wave receivers. You will see many rocks marked on this chart with a kind of asterisk having six points. Most of the rocks are close to shore, but some are isolated and in deeper water. These are ones to look out for.

As you begin to sail, and start to use your compasses, use the inner compass rose, marked MAGNETIC. Later you will learn to use the outer compass rose, on which true north is marked with a five-pointed star.

Stay clear of rocky places altogether.

Using your chart, plan the beginning of your sail. Since you are at a mooring, you can sail away with ease if you take a few precautions. Figure out exactly where you want to sail to on your first tack. If the harbor or the lake isn't crowded with a lot of boats in motion, you can make a general plan, which will take you to a place where you are in the clear and can practice sailing.

Put on the Sails

Unbag the mainsail. Slide the *battens* — strips of wood or plastic used to stiffen the *leech* of a sail — into their proper pockets. Battens seldom are all the same length. Make sure you match the length of the batten to the

Unbagging the mainsail in a Blue Jay.

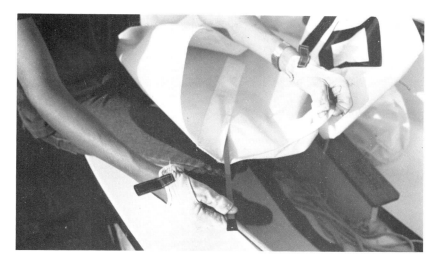

Putting a batten into the mainsail.

pocket. Forcing battens into pockets that aren't big enough for them will tear your sail, or at least rip a seam.

Using the diagrams of sails in this book, find the *foot* — the bottom edge of the sail. Take the *clew* — the *after* corner of the sail — and insert it into the slot on the boom. Near the mast, there will be a wider place, called a *gate*, where you can do this. Some old boats are equipped with tracks and metal fittings on the sail. However your boat is equipped, you will see what to do. Slide the clew from the gate, near the mast, toward the end of the boom.

If you have one, take away the *boom crutch,* a wooden crutch that supports the boom when the sail is not in use. Make sure the sheet isn't snarled so that when you pull the sail up, your boat won't begin to sail before you want it to. Cleat the sheet near its end if you want to, and make sure you have tied a figure-eight knot at the end of any sheet or halyard that leads through a *block* — a pulley consisting of a frame containing grooved rollers, over and around which lines run.

Make the foot of the mainsail as taut as is practical. Do this by first securing the *tack* of the sail to a point near the mast at the *gooseneck fitting* — the fitting which fastens the boom to the mast and allows it to swivel. Then pull the foot of the sail toward the end of the boom, and using what is called the *outhaul* — a light line attached to the clew of the sail, which is used to pull the foot of the sail taut — stretch the foot of the sail until it is taut but not so much that it will distort the sail. These and most other fittings vary widely, boat to boat, but if you know where they are and what purposes they serve, you will soon see how to use them.

Putting on foot of mainsail, inserting slides in track.

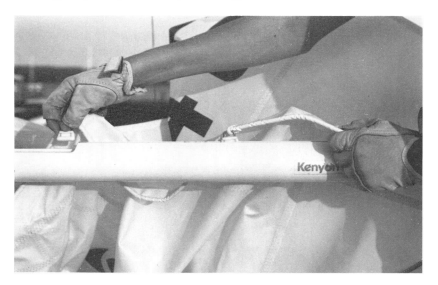

Boom crutch in place.

When the foot of the mainsail is in order, wrap two *stops* — narrow bands of cloth, lengths of line, or shock cord — around the sail so it won't blow overboard as you do other things.

Unbag the jib and sort it out. If the sheets are already attached to the clew, so much the better. If not, tie them both to the clew with a bowline, the knot used on larger boats in which the sheets are left in place and the sails are changed quite often. When the jib is ready to be put

Detail showing a gooseneck fitting with the downhaul attached and jam cleats on the mast.

onto the *forestay* — the wire leading from the bow to the masthead — leave the jib in the cockpit and proceed to raise the mainsail.

As you attach its halyard to the *head* — the topmost corner of the sail — make absolutely sure it is fastened properly to the sail. Most shackles are designed to lock into place somehow. As important as it is to check the shackle carefully, it is no less important to make sure the other end, the one you will hold in your hand when you raise the sail, won't get away from you and rise up out of reach. If either end escapes from you, you may be out of luck. You may see your halyard dangling, useless, high above you while your sail lies at your feet.

Once the shackle is secure, feed the *luff* — the leading edge of the sail — into the slot or track on the mast, starting with its head. Pulling slowly on the halyard, raise the sail, making sure it doesn't foul in the rigging — in the port or starboard shrouds or the backstay if you have one. Some boats are equipped with *spreaders* — more or less horizontal struts on the mast which are high above the deck and separate the shrouds from each other and the mast. Mainsails often catch in spreaders. If, as you raise the sail, you make sure the bow of your boat is pointing toward the wind, chances are the sail won't catch on anything.

As you raise the mainsail slowly, it will help you if your mate holds the boom up high enough to release the tension on the *leech* — the trailing edge of the sail. When you have pulled the halyard tight and cleated it, pull the *downhaul* and secure it so the luff won't sag and wrinkle.

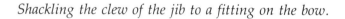

Shackling the clew of the jib to a fitting on the bow.

Leading the head of the mainsail into the track by pulling halyard gently and slowly.

The downhaul in place, fed through a jam cleat. Once the mainsail has been raised, its luff can be flattened slightly by pulling downward and securing this short length of line.

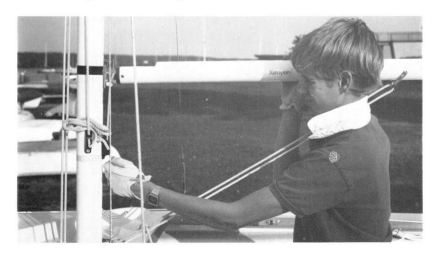

Putting the jib on the forestay with snap shackles. After you have shackled the tack of the jib to the fitting on the bow, start with the bottom snap shackle and work upward.

The downhaul is a light line that is tied below the gooseneck fitting, which when tightened pulls the boom down slightly.

As you bend on your sails, remember that their shape is what makes you go to windward. Their designer has spent hours, maybe weeks or even years, making drawings of their shapes. The fabric of your sails, which determines their weight and their elasticity, has been chosen with great care. Respect your sails as you handle them and use them.

Starting with its tack, put on the jib. In this case, it is easier to start with a lower corner so that gravity won't

work against you. Most jibs these days have *jib hanks* —
a kind of snap hook — on their luffs, which go around
the forestay. There are other kinds of rigs, twin slots on
forestays, things like that. Most rigs can be figured out
at a glance.

When the jib is secured to the forestay, attach its
halyard, again being careful that its shackle is secured
exactly as it should be. Raise the jib, pulling firmly. On
some boats, the jib halyard can be winched up, but on
most boats under eighteen feet there are no winches. On
small boats, you can sweat the halyard up. Lead it around
the bottom of the cleat, pulling hard, and when you can
pull no more, keep tension on it with one hand. Grasp

*Jib halyard fed through a block to a cleat. This picture demonstrates
how to wrap and lock line around a cleat and how to coil and hang
the line.*

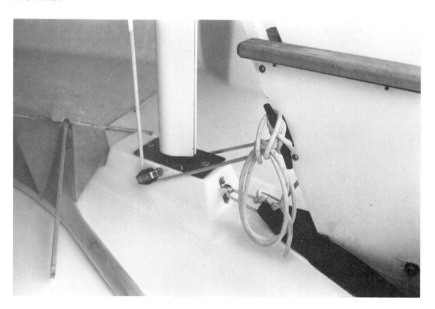

the halyard a foot or so above the cleat with your free hand, pulling outward, and release it suddenly, at the same time pulling it around the cleat. In this way, you can gain an inch or two.

Casting Off

Now the sails are up and flapping. Even on a light air day, the sounds of sails cracking and snapping can be most intimidating, but once trimmed, they will make so little noise that you will hear the whisper of the water as your boat makes her way.

As your mate gets ready to cast off, you are sitting with a hand on the tiller. You have the mainsheet in your hand so as you sail you can ease it instantly, spilling wind if necessary. Spilling wind will of course slow your boat, and bring it to an even keel, but remember, forward motion gives you what control you have. A boat drifting aimlessly is prey to sudden gusts of wind and vagrant currents. Forward motion will put you in command.

Your mate is standing at the bow, ready to let go of the mooring pendant on the side away from which you plan to sail. This procedure will prevent your boat from running over it, so your centerboard or rudder won't become entangled in it.

As you start, remember that the points of sailing as defined in diagrams seem distinct from one another but are parts of a continuum. Let's say you plan to sail away on a *port tack* — with the wind coming from the left-hand side of your boat — and *close-hauled*. You can wait until your boat is heading more or less where you want it to and then direct your mate to let the mooring pendant

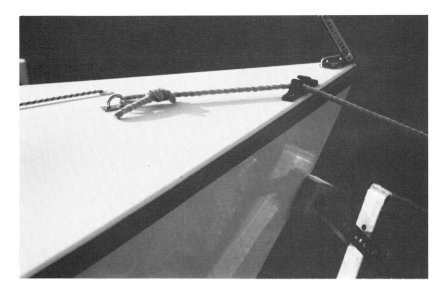

Detail showing a bow pendant fed through a bow chock and made fast to a bow fitting with a bowline.

and the dinghy go. It will help if your mate holds the clew of the jib out to port, so the wind will move the bow to starboard. This is called *backing the jib*. In any case, when your heading satisfies you, tell your mate to drop the pendant, trim your sails, and off you go!

Under Way

Following the plan you've made, steer clear of all obstructions — boats at moorings, docks, rocks, other sailboats. As you go, keep on holding the mainsheet in your hand. Your mate can manage the jib sheets.

Remember, when you want to slow down, ease the

sheets until the sail is *luffing*, or spilling wind. In tight quarters, as you pass boats at moorings or at anchor, ask your mate to be alert to fend off with hands or feet. There is no shame nor is there any danger in avoiding a collision in this way. After all, your boat is light. When you sail in larger boats, however, never do this. If you do, you might lose a hand or foot.

If your mate is busy fending off, or doing other things, you can handle both the mainsheet and the jib sheets. In fact, as part of learning to work well together, you and your mate should take turns sailing without each other's help so both of you will know your boat and can sail her if one of you falls overboard.

On your first day, it will be tempting to sail to a far objective, jibe or come about, and go back home, but you won't learn to sail this way. Looking at the diagrams of points of sailing, practice everything.

As you go, make use of your centerboard. It helps you keep your course without slipping sideways. It should be extended when you are sailing close-hauled and be up when you are running. On a *beam reach*, it should be between the two positions and so on. There will be times when you are running when you will want the board down just a little.

Water pressure on the centerboard can make it stick. If you try to lower it and this happens, luff a little. This will probably free it.

As you are learning, sit always on the windward side. It's fun to *heel* — tip — your boat, but your rudder and your sails will work better if you heel only slightly. Heeling sharply cannot always be avoided, but it's not productive. Later on, in strong winds, you and your mate will have to *hike out* — to lean out to windward — in

Points of sailing on a port tack. From the left: close-hauled, close reach, beam reach, broad reach, run. These terms are the same on both port and starboard tacks. Close-hauled is always closest to the wind.

order to avoid capsizing, so now, on this light air day, learn to use hiking straps, if you have them.

Remember the wind indicators. Use the ones which work for you. Some telltales act as flags or banners do but indicate apparent wind. Bits of thread poked through the jib work exactly as do plastic ribbons which are attached to a window in the jib. The port ribbon is red and the starboard one is green. When the sail is drawing as it should, the ribbons are parallel, streaming straight back toward the leech, the after corner of the sail. Sailing on a starboard tack, if the green ribbon drops below the horizontal, the sail is luffing slightly. If the green ribbon rises and the red one drops, the sail itself will look pretty much the same as it did when you were sailing properly but indicates that you are sailing *off the wind*, that you could point a little *higher* — closer to the wind. When you race, these fine points become important. As you learn, they are less so, but if you always strive for good sail trim, you will become a safer, better sailor.

Let's assume that you have sailed to a place where you are in the clear, where you have room to maneuver. Start close-hauled. Give a generous portion of your time to practicing this point of sailing.

Put your board all the way down. Trim the mainsail and the jib so they match; so their luffs point directly toward the wind, at the same time that your bow is 45° or so off the wind. When you think you're moving well,

How hiking straps are used.

Sailing close-hauled. In small centerboarders, even when the wind is light, hiking out is necessary to maintain good hull trim.

pick a landmark or a buoy and sail toward it, trimming sails for maximum efficiency. Trim your jib first. Holding course — in this case pointing straight toward your objective — ease the sheet until it luffs, trembles slightly and grows soft. Trim it in until it hardens. Now, using the same method, trim the mainsail.

Because of what is called the *slot effect* — the result of the flow of air between the mainsail and the jib — the two sails compliment each other. As I say, trim your jib first. The behavior of the mainsail is determined at least partly by the slot effect. Bear in mind that if your jib is overtrimmed — trimmed too tightly — it will make your mainsail luff.

When you are sailing close-hauled, it is the shape of your sails that is pulling you forward. Your sails are more sophisticated instruments than the sails of old square-rigged ships. Close-hauled, when they are working as they should, the wind is acting on them as it acts on the shape of an airplane wing. The air divides or separates as it approaches the leading edge of a wing. Because an airplane wing is shaped the way it is, the air on top must travel farther, faster than the air that flows along the underside. This reduces the air pressure on the top, which in turn produces lift.

When you are sailing close-hauled, your sails, which might be described as airplane wings in a vertical position, produce more or less the same effect as wings. The

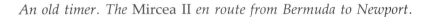

An old timer. The Mircea II *en route from Bermuda to Newport.*

action of the wind produces horizontal lift, which, in concert with the counteraction of the centerboard or keel, produces forward motion, sometimes at angles less than 45° to the wind. This special force diminishes as you go from sailing close-hauled to a *reach* — all points of sailing between running and close-hauled — and disappears as you begin to sail downwind.

When your sails are drawing well, sailing close-hauled can be thrilling, even on a light air day. Your boat heels, sometimes sharply, and you feel wind on your face. As your boat knifes through the water, it seems to pulse and bound, making gentle hissing sounds.

Now, before you have to tack, think about what you will do. Let's suppose that you are sailing in a north wind — a wind coming from the north — close-hauled, on a port tack, heading toward a buoy. In this case, when

Hiking out.

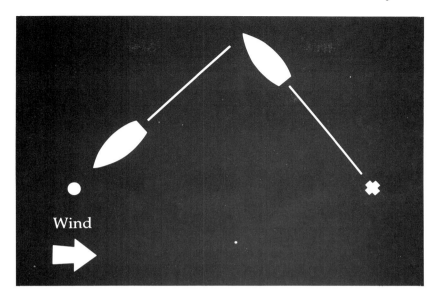

This diagram shows a boat tacking to a point windward by starting off on a port tack, tacking once, and then approaching the objective on a starboard tack.

you tack, you will make your bow swing sharply to the left. Your new course will be roughly 90° — at right angles — to the one you're sailing now. Make a guess as to where you will be heading after you have come about. Pick something you will be heading toward on your new tack — another buoy or a landmark. Tell your mate exactly what you plan to do. If the wind comes in puffs, wait for a patch of stronger wind before you start to make your move. Before you tack, ask your mate if he or she is ready, saying "Ready about?"

Your mate should nod or answer, "Ready."

Then as you push the tiller away from you, say, "Hard alee!" Move the tiller quickly, firmly. Watch your bow swing around toward the second buoy or the land-mark. At the same time, move across the boat, from port to starboard, taking a new position from which you will steer the boat. Good sailors move with a fair degree of grace, in a natural, fluid way. Beginners often lunge and move in jerks. Gracefulness will come with practice. As you swing the boat to windward, your mate will let go of the jib sheet on the leeward side, take hold of the other sheet, and, as the jib luffs, pull the port sheet in and cleat it temporarily. As the boom swings across, duck your head if necessary. When you take up your new course, your mate will trim or ease the sheet so you can gather speed again.

If you find it difficult to come about, swing back to your former course, gather speed, and try again. Re-member, you can't come about without *way* — or for-ward motion. If you find yourself in this predicament, ease the sheets and back the jib, as you did when you set sail. If you can see and feel which way the wind is coming from, you will know which way to coax the boat to go.

No matter what your new course is, if you have room, come about once again. Do this repeatedly. Pick a place directly upwind. Tack toward it on what will be a zigzag course, and as you approach the mark on your next to last tack, sail a little past the point where you think you have to tack to fetch it. This will give you what some sailors call *money in the bank.* Doing this, you will approach your mark with ease, instead of *pinching* — luffing, moving sluggishly. Practice tacking tirelessly, as when skiing you might practice countless turns. Soon, you will know exactly how to judge the wind and sea and come about with perfect ease.

Sailing on a broad reach, in light airs.

When you are *beating* — sailing close-hauled toward a mark — and you ease sheets, changing course a few degrees, you are sailing on a *close reach*. On a *beam reach*, you are sailing more or less at right angles to the wind, and as you continue changing course and easing sheets, approaching what is called a *run,* you are sailing a *broad reach*. I won't define these points of sailing in the text. A diagram can do it best, but remember as you sail that all points of sailing fit together and become a single, fluid operation.

On any reach, you can maneuver better and faster than you can when you are beating. Incidentally, that is why a sailboat close-hauled has the right of way over boats that are reaching or are sailing *downwind* — more or less with the wind.

On a close reach, you may be a little drier than when sailing close-hauled, but you will heel as much or more. As before, hike out to keep your *hull trimmed* decently — to keep it on a more or less even keel.

A beam reach is the fastest point of sailing. On a beam reach, you are using both the simple pushing action of the wind, and its lift. A beam reach is almost always comfortable. There are times when you can't make concessions to the wind, but when you can and you are looking for a drier, safer course, sail a reach.

A run can be a tricky point of sailing, especially in strong winds and feisty seas. When you run, you sometimes feel like a balloonist in the basket of a balloon, moving always with the wind, seeming almost motionless. When you are running properly, the wind will come across the *transom* — the stern facing of the hull — at one corner or the other, and you will have eased your mainsheet so the boom is nearly at right angles to the wind. Incidentally, at no time should the boom invade the foredeck — that portion of the deck which lies forward of the mast.

On a broad reach or a run, you must be constantly alert, watching every indication of the wind's direction — telltales, masthead fly, and water — sailing to avoid a *jibe*. As you learn to sail downwind, you should understand what is meant by a jibe. If the wind is at your back as you face the boom and mainsail, which are on your right-hand side, and if you pull the mainsail in and steer slightly to your right, suddenly the sail will fill on the opposite side. This will swing the sail and boom across the boat with a sudden, violent motion.

If you do this in light winds, and do it carefully, intentionally, it can be a safe maneuver. In an accidental

The boat in front is between a broad reach and a run; the other boat is sailing close-hauled.

jibe, the motion of the boom and sail can break a stay or shroud, sweep the rigging overboard, and leave you helpless, floundering. A poorly executed jibe can make your boat *broach* — swing broadside to the wind. In light winds, you can get away with broaching, but in strong winds it may cause you to capsize. Incidentally, if your boat shows a tendency to broach, bring weight *aft* — toward the back of the boat — so as to reduce the fishtail action of your hull. Just as a jibe can cause a broach, so a broach can can cause a jibe.

I once witnessed what an accidental jibe can do. I was sailing with five other people from Fort Lauderdale to Newport in late March, aboard a racing boat. As we set sail, the air was warm, the water green. Winds were moderate and steady, promising a happy passage, but grew stronger as we sailed and at last, as we approached Cape Hatteras, they were blowing very hard, up to forty miles an hour. Seas began to dwarf the boat. Three of us began to reef — to shorten the amount of sail exposed to the wind. Suddenly, the boat broached and we jibed. One man, carried with the boom, was catapulted toward the rail. For a moment he hung above the icy sea, reaching toward us. The boat rolled, giving him a moment's grace. Then, the crewman nearest to him grabbed his jacket, and pulled him back. Had the man fallen overboard, chances were he would have drowned.

Good habits, learned as you begin to sail, can help prevent near tragedies and deaths at sea. Sailing downwind, if your jib is full and working on the same side as your mainsail, you won't jibe. Watch your jib. Expect it to flutter slightly now and then, but when it wants to cross the foredeck and fill on the opposite side, change course slightly, heading back toward a broad reach, in order to avoid a jibe.

Your boat is probably equipped with a *boom vang* — a line that runs from the mast at deck level to a point on the boom which might be one-third of the way from the mast to the end of the boom. When you run, adjust the vang and cleat it firmly. The vang helps hold down the boom, on a broad reach or a run. This keeps the mainsail flat, increases speed, and helps prevent a jibe. If the boom rises far above the horizontal, the mainsail begins to belly, spilling wind, making its shape less efficient.

The boat you are sailing may or may not be equipped with a third sail, a *spinnaker*. This sail, designed to give you extra speed downwind and on reaches, is a tricky sail to use. If you have one, leave it in its bag awhile, for

Sailing downwind under spinnakers.

two or three months at least, until you have mastered
sailing under main and working jib. Keep it dry and
maybe air it now and then. When you are ready for a
spinnaker, you will find countless books that will tell you
how to use it. I have seen at least one book — *Spinnaker*
by R. "Bunty" King* — which is devoted entirely to instruction in the use of spinnakers and the gear that goes
with them. As you gain skill and confidence, you may
want to *wing your jib* — prop it out with a light pole on
the opposite side from the mainsail — as you go to windward, but for now, as you learn to sail, be content to
leave the jib free so that it can warn you of a jibe
impending.

* *Spinnaker* was published in Great Britain by Fakenham Press, Fakenham,
Norfolk, and in America by Sail Books, 34 Commercial Wharf, Boston,
Massachusetts 02110.

When you feel altogether comfortable sailing downwind, try an intentional jibe. You should jibe only if the wind is light. Before you jibe, bring the mainsheet in slowly, and begin to change course for the jibe. The jib will flap and cross the deck with a kind of whacking sound, but the mainsail won't give you this kind of warning. All at once, the wind will slap the sail and boom across. As it does so, take up your new course, which will be 25° or so from your old one.

When you are heading downward toward a mark, it is sometimes more efficient and a little safer if you execute several intentional jibes. If you jibe repeatedly, taking a zigzag course, you are doing what is called *jibing downwind*. In light airs, this is safe but when in doubt go from a run to a broad reach, then to a beam reach, then a close reach, and finally sail close-hauled and come about. Remember, when you come about from a run or any kind of reach, head up slowly on successive points of sail until you are close-hauled, then, as you gather

Jibing downwind.

Wind

Shackling the main halyard to the head of the sail.

Town and city governments have sailing schools in public parks. The Charles River Basin, Boston, Massachusetts.

Docking a Blue Jay.

Quiet day under way.

Neck and neck.

Dave Bridges at the Sobstad loft working on a template for a Blue Jay mainsail.

Sailmaking is an art. Sobstad Sail Loft, Old Saybrook, Connecticut.

Rolling the mainsail.

Sailors spend a lot of time looking up.

Jim Johnstone and Clifford Gurnham winning on a light air day.

Even keel.

*The author at the helm of
an ocean racing boat.*

speed, come about. In doing so, you will be describing a half circle.

Now try what sailing expert Steve Colgate calls a circle of courses. If you can find a stretch of water large enough that is protected and unobstructed, sail around in a full circle, both clockwise and counterclockwise, practicing all points of sailing. This drill will help you learn to move around the boat and to adjust the centerboard. If you do it many times, trimming sail will become almost second nature to you.

Shooting

As you master basic skills, you must learn to retrieve a mate who has fallen overboard. With this in mind, practice *shooting* — coasting up to an object in the water. This is perhaps the single most important skill for you to learn. It is dangerous to approach someone directly under sail. Though it may seem inefficient, shooting up to them is best.

Practice shooting. Throw a life vest or a buoyant cushion overboard and, using it as a target, practice ghosting up to it. You and your mate must both take turns at the tiller so you both will know how this is done. With a stopwatch, you can time these exercises.

Simply stated, shooting is the art of judging just how far your boat will go once her sails become inactive. When you shoot, it is as if you started tacking and stopped turning as you faced the wind directly. It is clear that when you face a stronger wind you will coast a shorter distance than you will in a light wind. Even though your sails aren't working, a strong wind will blow you backward.

Practice shooting from all points of sailing. From a run, push down your centerboard, sail a reach, then sail close-hauled, come about, and approach your target at an angle, aiming for a point below it. This imaginary point represents the place from which you think you can coast up to your target without benefit of sail. Practice coming alongside the life vest as you would if it were a living person.

If you are on a reach or are close-hauled when you toss the vest overboard, push down your centerboard, jibe about, and sail back toward the same imaginary point. As you approach it, harden up and sail close-hauled before you shoot up to your target. As you snuggle up to it, you must lose way altogether. As you do this, let your sheets run. If you don't, your boat may start to sail again.

Some skippers recommend that you aim for a position just downwind of your target, so you won't drift down on it. Others say that it is best to arrive slightly upwind of your target so it won't be out of reach if you don't fetch it. Practice doing both and make a choice depending on the circumstances. Size of a boat and strength of wind are factors that are critical. In a small boat, you will probably decide to lose way upwind of your target. In any case, if you practice many times, you will make the right decision.

If on the first of several tries, you miss your target altogether, there's no need to reach for it. Relax. Leave it lying in the water. Try again, and then again. Shoot up to it repeatedly, and when at last you pick it up, use your boat hook.

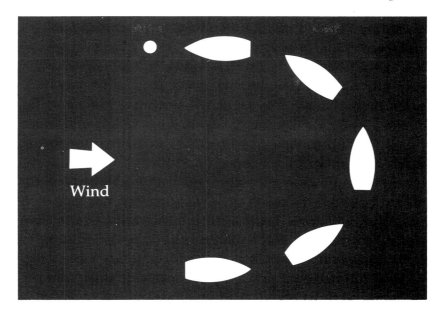

Shooting up to an object in the water.

Having learned the trick of shooting, you can now perform a rescue. Especially when you first learn to sail, the risks are high that one of you — you or your mate — will tumble overboard, maybe stunned by a boom as it swings across your boat, or after slipping on the deck. In all cases, strive to think and act efficiently.

If someone does fall overboard, first call, "Man overboard!" As you do this, throw a life vest, lifejacket, life ring, or cushion to the person in the water. Shout a word of reassurance. DON'T JUMP IN. Shoot up to them.

There have been dramatic cases, on the high seas, when a sailor has jumped overboard to rescue someone in the water. Charles F. Tillinghast, Jr., was at the helm of the *Hamrah*, racing from Bermuda to Norway, when owner-skipper Robert Ames was caught up by a giant wave and swept into the sea. Tillinghast yelled for the men below and started an intentional jibe.

Robert Ames's sons, Richard and Henry, were aboard the *Hamrah*. Richard came on deck, seized a line which had been purposely left at the stern, in case of a mishap. He jumped. The line wasn't long enough. Richard couldn't reach his father. He let go of the line and started swimming toward him. Mr. Ames, weighted down by boots and heavy clothing, was by now close to sinking. His head was barely visible.

Tillinghast, maneuvering as well as he could, finished jibing the *Hamrah*. He said later, "I tried to shoot up to the people in the water, in an effort to get as close as possible without losing too much headway.

"We got to possibly fifteen feet of them but, as we drew nearer, a steep wave pushed them out of reach."

Following a series of mishaps aboard the *Hamrah*, including the breaking of the main boom, Robert Ames's second son launched a boat and rowed to his brother. By this time, Mr. Ames was lost.

Now Tillinghast had a crew of only two left on board.

As Richard climbed aboard the rowboat, the frail little craft began to ship water. Tillinghast tried to sail the crippled *Hamrah* to windward to rescue the boys, but the rowboat sank and Tillinghast could no longer see the boys. After spending hours searching, hoping for a miracle, Tillinghast and his remaining crew decided to ride out the gale. Every shred of hope was gone.

At sea, jumping overboard is little better than committing suicide and most times it doesn't help. *STAY WITH YOUR BOAT.* Had the Ames boys stayed aboard the *Hamrah*, Mr. Ames would have had as good a chance or better of surviving and his sons would not have drowned. As it was, all three were lost.

Remember, as you shoot up to a swimmer, take care not to sail straight at him. Let the sheets run, so the boat won't sail away, and if they are out of reach, throw them a life preserver, come around, and try again.

Anchoring

Anchoring is part of sailing. Unless you have a Sunfish, Laser, sailboard, or similar small boat, you should never sail without an anchor. In strong and unexpected winds when you have to douse your sails, you will be at the mercy of the weather. Short wooden paddles won't propel you very far. There is a chance, a small one, that the wind will blow you, without sails, to a safe place. If it won't, you must anchor. You will also use an anchor when you want to leave your boat unattended.

You will almost certainly be equipped with a 6- or 8-pound Danforth or a similar small anchor having thin sharp *flukes*, which will dig in on whichever side the anchor rests, and a length of half-inch nylon line.

This line, or rode, should be tied with a *round turn* — an extra loop — and a bowline. Check the bowline to make sure you have tied it properly. The anchor must be somehow tied to your boat so it won't fall overboard.

Some sailing books recommend that you carry 175 feet of anchor rode for every 25 feet of water you may anchor in — a ratio of seven to one. In a small boat, you can choke yourself to death on two hundred feet or so of anchor rode. At best, you will clutter your small boat.

Admitting that it isn't always wise or even possible to let your boat drift into shallow water before you drop your anchor, I still recommend that you carry no more than 100 feet of nylon anchor rode and that you mark it somehow so that you will know how much line you are spending as you pay it out.

If you shackle a short length of chain between the anchor and the rode, your holding power will increase and you can anchor faster since the chain will help the anchor sink and will keep it lying flat. This chain must be shackled properly to both rode and anchor. Any ship's store worth its weight in salt will assemble these components for you. Later on, if you learn marlin spike seamanship, you can assemble them yourself.

Before you approach the place where you will anchor, make fast the end of your anchor rode, as you did your towing line, around the mast or bow cleat, passing it through your bow *chock* — the guide fitting on the bow. Pick your spot, remembering that your boat will drift to leeward as you drop your anchor and as it takes hold. If you can sail without it, douse your jib, and take it off if possible. This will clear the foredeck and will keep the jib in shape. Also, sails don't make good footing. They are slippery.

Shoot up to the place where you plan to drop the anchor. Lower it. Never throw it. Throwing it may snarl the rope or, worse, wrap the rope around your leg and take you overboard.

In five feet of water pay out twenty feet or so of anchor rode, in ten feet of water, forty feet, and so on. A ratio of four to one is adequate. Later on, when you sail in heavy weather, you will carry much more line,

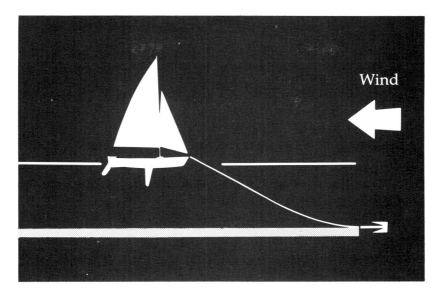

When anchoring, shoot up to the place you want the anchor to dig in, drop it gently overboard, let the boat drift to leeward, and pay out as much anchor rode as you need. Test the anchor to make sure it is holding.

and aboard larger boats, you may carry several anchors, each designed for a special kind of bottom.

Pay out anchor rode slowly. Let your boat drift back on it, taking up slack as it goes. You will know when it takes hold. When you are securely anchored, douse the mainsail. Furl it.

When you leave your anchorage, raise your sails, and, keeping all sheets slack, slowly pull your boat to windward, toward the anchor. When your bow is directly over it, you can break the anchor out with a minimum of effort.

Dunk the anchor several times, to clean off bottom sediment, and if necessary scrub it. Coil its rode and store it carefully before you set sail again.

Undocking and Docking

The best docks are equipped with strips of rubber or plastic or padded canvas rails which protect boats docking at them. Large boats always carry *fenders* — soft, elongated, balloonlike objects that crew members hang between the dock and the boat. I won't recommend that you carry fenders at all times, but if your dock is not protected, you may want to carry small ones or some kind of substitute. In tidal waters, the best docks of all for small boats are floating docks, which rise and fall as the water level does.

When docking and undocking, you must know exactly where the wind is coming from. This is the key to relaxed, successful docking operations, for both sailboats and boats under power. Some time ago, I spent time aboard a tug. Powerful as tugs are, their captains know that they must reckon with the wind, especially when they dock and undock ships that present vast surfaces to whatever wind is blowing. Your boat, even with no sails aloft, is affected by the wind. Many boats are capable of "sailing" without sails, with the wind and sometimes when the wind is abeam.

The thought of docking makes a lot of people nervous. How many times have you seen a skipper who lacks confidence yelling at the people on his deck who stand ready with the lines? The secret is to take things

Docking at the Watch Hill Yacht Club in Watch Hill, Rhode Island.

easy and as often as you can let the wind do the work. This is doubly true for you in your small boat. After all, as I suggested earlier, you can use your hands and feet for fending off.

If the wind is blowing you against your dock and you want to sail away, you can walk your boat around to a place where the wind will take you clear. Remember, if you want to raise your sails before you leave the dock, your bow must be pointing to windward. Avoid positions where the wind will blow your sails against the pilings or the dock.

If you can't walk your boat around, you had better paddle out to a place where you can anchor and put on your sails at your leisure.

If the wind is blowing you off the dock, if you will be running or broad reaching as you sail away, you might leave a stern line on, let your bow drift out to leeward, bend on your sails, raise them, let go of the line, and shove off, taking care not to jibe.

During all these maneuvers, you will have to use your docking lines with intelligence and care. Looking at my diagram of the four docking lines, learn their names, and figure out which lines to release first and last, when the wind is coming from a variety of points.

When you undock, your primary concern is making way, sailing clear, not being blown back to the dock. As you do in all other situations — plan, then act. If the wind is blowing toward the dock face where you want to dock, things become more difficult than they would be otherwise. If practical, shoot up to a point to wind-ward of the dock, douse your sails, and let the wind take

If the wind is not too strong and you position fenders carefully, spring lines will be needed only if you plan to leave boat unattended. This picture shows a dock equipped with cleats. Pilings work just as well.

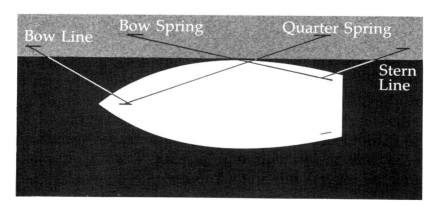

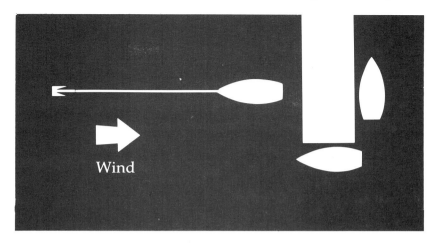

In strong winds, you can anchor 40 feet or so offshore, and pay out your anchor line while the wind blows your boat toward a dock. This leaves your anchor out to windward but is practical for temporary docking.

you down on the dock face. This works well if the wind is not too strong.

In strong winds that blow you toward a dock, you can anchor 40 feet or so offshore, and pay out your anchor line while the wind blows your boat toward a dock. This leaves your anchor out to windward but is practical for temporary docking, to leave off or pick up someone. It also makes departing easier. Hand over hand, you can pull yourself back out.

If a wind opposite to the one I've just described is blowing you off the dock, pick a place on the dock where you can take hold and shoot up to it, losing way as you reach it, tie a line around a piling, with a clove hitch, or cleat the line if possible, and then stream away to leeward as you douse your sails and sort things out.

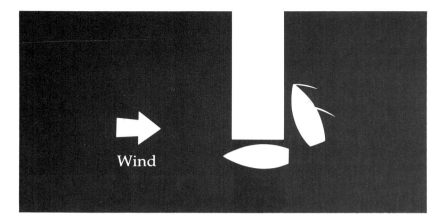

Docking on the leeward side of the dock. You should approach the dock luffing, and use the remaining "way" to swing parallel to the dock.

A light boat presents few docking problems.

If the wind is blowing parallel to the face of the dock, you can shoot up to a point beside it, snuggle up, and let your sheets run. In every case, if you make use of the wind, you will succeed.

Running Aground

Writer first and sailor second, I must often bow to other sailors, some my seniors, some my juniors — but I count myself an expert when it comes to running *shoal-draft* sailboats hard aground on sandy bottoms.

Not long ago, I wrote an article about a catboat cruise I took with the object of exploring places not accessible to deep-draft boats — large keel-boats, which run aground in shallow places. With a mate, I sailed among the islands south of Cape Cod. Though we drew less than two feet with our centerboard up, we ran aground several times, under favorable conditions. One time, as the waters were receding, we were stranded on a sandbar seven hours. In a smaller, lighter boat, we could easily have shoved off, but though our boat was only 18 feet L.O.A. — length overall — she weighed 2,200 pounds, so we just relaxed and watched as she went high and dry. As it happened, we were on an island that was uninhabited and we had a good time there, walking, swimming, taking pictures of the birds, one of which was a large goose.

I'm glad to say that I have never hit a rock. I have seen what rocks can do to hulls of boats and have managed to avoid them. I have been with other sailors when they hit rocks and continued sailing, shrugging. Once, I saw a large sailboat hung up on a pile of rocks. If winds are light, the tide is low, and seas are flat, some boats can survive a mishap such as this, but if a sea is running, the boat will pound against the rocks until she springs a leak and starts to fill. On a beach, I once saw the jagged shards of what had been the hull of a fiberglass sailboat. A sight like that is a reminder of the power of the sea.

Stay away from shallow places unless they are in sheltered, tranquil waters ringed with sandy beaches. If the waters where you sail abound in islands, and have beaches free of rocks, you can run your boat ashore, take a swim, and stay awhile. If you do this, walk your anchor to a point above the high water mark and set it firmly in the sand. If the tide is rising, watch your boat even though you've set your anchor.

Most times, you'd rather not run aground and sometimes you know it would be downright dangerous. If

Sailing into shallow waters.

your boat has a centerboard and it is down, it will warn you of impending danger. You will hear and feel it strike the bottom. It will rise in its trunk. If this happens, raise the centerboard and retreat, as you would if someone had just fallen overboard. If possible, jibe about. Sailing on will probably put you aground.

If you do run hard aground and can't sail off, raise the centerboard, take off the rudder, and ease all sheets. On a sandy, shallow bottom, maybe you and your mate can push the boat off. Only in very shallow water will this work. Before you jump out of the boat, make sure that you can climb aboard when you have finished push-ing. Carefully judge the water's depth. It may be deeper than you think, or may suddenly shelve off. Wear life vests, and if there is any chance that either of you will have trouble going back aboard your boat, leave some-body in the cockpit. If both of you push the boat, secure it somehow to your person with a line, so it won't get away from you.

If it isn't practical to walk your boat to deeper waters and to climb back aboard, maybe you can swim your anchor into deeper waters, but before you leave your boat, cleat the end of its line so that if you drop the anchor you won't lose it. If it seems necessary, buoy your small anchor with a life vest or life ring.

Back aboard your grounded boat, take up the slack on the rode very gently, as if you were trying to land a fish. If the anchor digs in firmly, pull or winch the anchor rode in slowly, hoping you can work your boat free. Move your weight to a point above the deepest water. It may help to rock the boat from side to side.

If these methods fail to work, hail a boat capable of towing you. If your boat has a bow cleat that won't break or pull away under stress, cleat a line at the bow and lead it through the bow chock — and coil it so you can hand or toss it to your rescuer. Incidentally, if you plan to heave it, tie a bowline at its end, to give the end weight, and coil it near the knotted end. Make a second, looser coil to hold in your nonthrowing hand.

If your boat has no bow cleat, tie the line around the mast near the deck. Hand or heave the line exactly as you would have had you secured it to a cleat. It is often better for the skipper of the smaller vessel to supply the towing line. The skipper of a large powerboat will probably provide a line too thick to go around your cleat or through your chock. It is hard to give advice to someone who is being kind to you, but if the towing skipper isn't careful ask him to please to be so, so he won't pull out your cleat or dismast your boat. In open water, he will have to take it easy or your boat will travel at a speed greater than what is called *hull speed* — the theoretical maximum speed of the hull (the square root of her length at her waterline multiplied by 1.4). If she is towed at greater speeds, she will *plow* — drive her bow below the surface of the water. Some sailboats can exceed hull speed, when they sail before the wind and *plane* — skim along on the surface of the water. When you are in deeper water, your rescuer will set you loose and return your line to you.

Capsizing

Armed with knowledge, there is no need to fear capsizing. In fact, the best way to prepare for a capsize is to capsize purposely several times and learn what moves to make. If you do this, pick a mild day and a place where the water is a little deeper than your mast is long.

Before you sailed, you checked your flotation tanks and covered them. As it should be, your equipment is secure in canvas pouches or in watertight containers, which are tied down. Your boat hook, paddles, extra life vests, and flotation cushions won't float free. Your horn is where you can find it easily, and your anchor is secured.

You must be wearing your life vests so you are buoyant and won't tire as easily as you would if you were swimming while you worked. Saving life must be your first consideration. When you capsize, find your mate. Make sure he or she has not been stunned and is not on the verge of drowning.

Let's assume that your boat is lying on her side, with her mainsail and her jib flat against the water. If at first you fail to see your mate, look underneath the sails. If it is you who is underneath a sail, you will have air and light and can easily work your way out from under. Chances are, both of you are floating nicely.

The best antidote to fear is to know what to do and go to work. The nearest land may look close, but it is almost certainly farther than it looks, and bear in mind that it is harder for a rescuer to see a person in the water than a boat. Your head is small and disappears among even modest waves.

If your boat is in a current or is drifting with the wind, keep a grip on a line or take a handhold on the boat. If you are in command, take one job and, speaking quietly, give your mate a job to do. Unless the water is quite flat and you are confident, don't take off your life vest and swim underwater, trying to find lines and equip-

A chase boat bailing a sailboat after it capsized.

ment, and in any case, do this only if you find that you can see well underwater and your mate is a good swimmer. This is no time for heroics.

Ask your mate to stand on the centerboard, near the hull not on its end, so as not to break it off. This will keep the boat from *turning turtle* — that is, rolling over all the way, so its mast is pointing downward. Take a life vest or a cushion and proceed along the mast to the masthead, and secure the life vest or cushion under it, tying it if possible.

Take down the sails — that is, pull them toward the hull and furl them roughly if you can — so that when you right the boat they won't knock you down again. Now, with your mate still standing on the centerboard, take the floating object off the mast and help your mate right the boat. Since it is full of water, it will be unstable. From your positions in the water, find a way to balance it while you bail with a bucket or your hands, sloshing water out of the cockpit faster than it comes back in. It is sometimes possible to move a swamped boat with a paddle, but not easily and not far. If bailing works, use a bucket, then a hand pump.

Most boats don't turn turtle. If your boat is bottom up, the rules are much the same as they would be if she were in a capsized attitude. If possible, uncleat the mainsheet so the sail won't provide unwanted drag against your efforts to bring the mast up to the point where it is lying on the surface of the water. Cleat or tie a line to one side of the boat and lead it across the bottom to the other side. Now you can brace your feet against the boat and, pulling on the line, try to right her. If you can't, secure a second line so you and your mate can pull on one. Bear in mind that in water shallower than your mast's length, the masthead may have lodged on the bottom. If it has, there may be nothing you can do but find handholds and wait for rescue. Don't spend your energy attempting the impossible.

Hand pump.

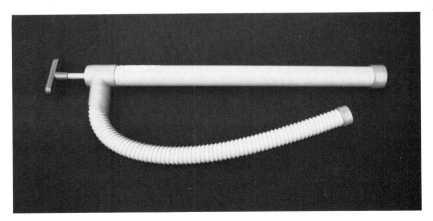

If you can't right your boat, talk to your mate about what your next move should be. In most cases, other boats will come to help you, but if you are not near other boats, sound your horn repeatedly or blow the whistle which is tied around your neck. If, after you repeat the signal many times and nobody comes, blow SOS. This is not accepted practice, but it will work. Blow three short sounds, three long sounds, and three short sounds. Each letter has a kind of beat and rhythm of its own. Strung together, they constitute a kind of tune. Use this signal only as a last resort and never blow it just for fun. If you do, it will bring a horde of rescuers, who will be angry as a flight of yellow jackets when they see what you have done. In any case, stay with your boat.

Since your boat will be swamped, whoever tows you must be sure to take up slack on the towline very slowly. If your mast is on the bottom, snagged or stuck, tell the towing skipper what the situation is so he will tow in such a way as not to bend the mast, but to free it. Crash boats often are equipped with powered winches so their crews can free a mast that has become lodged on the bottom.

A skipper towing a swamped boat must do so at a snail's pace. Otherwise, the boat may capsize several times before it reaches a safe place, where it can at last be bailed and put to rights. Back in port, remember that your boat has suffered trauma. After you have bailed her dry, check her flotation tanks. Check her rigging. Hose her down. Wash and dry her sails, fold and bag them. In fact, even after routine jaunts your boat and sails deserve a lot of tender, loving care.

Venturing

I had skippered my own boat five years or so when I wrote to an English broker asking for some information about a small *double-ended* sailboat capable of making ocean voyages. I thought I might buy the boat with a friend and sail her south from England to the Canary Islands, and across to the West Indies, then to the United States, using prevailing winds and ocean currents.

My dream was almost within reach, but as it happened, I spent several years more sailing my small boat, pushing myself very slowly.

As you develop confidence, you will leave familiar waters. Probably your small boat won't have bunks, but you can sail and camp.

Let's imagine you are spending several weeks in August on the coast of Martha's Vineyard, a large Massachusetts island. You have trailed your boat along and you keep her in a harbor near your house.

Your bedroom overlooks the water and at night you see a flashing light which must be five miles or so from where you live. You have heard that the light comes from a lighthouse on a bluff on Cape Poge, a pleasant place, secluded even in the summer. You decide to pick a time when the forecast promises light winds and sunny skies, sail to Cape Poge with a tent and some food, spend a night, and sail back home. You buy a large-scale chart, representing a small part of the earth's surface which includes both your harbor and Cape Poge. As you study it, you see that you will have to sail southeast, to a place called Cape Poge Gut, a narrow channel which appears

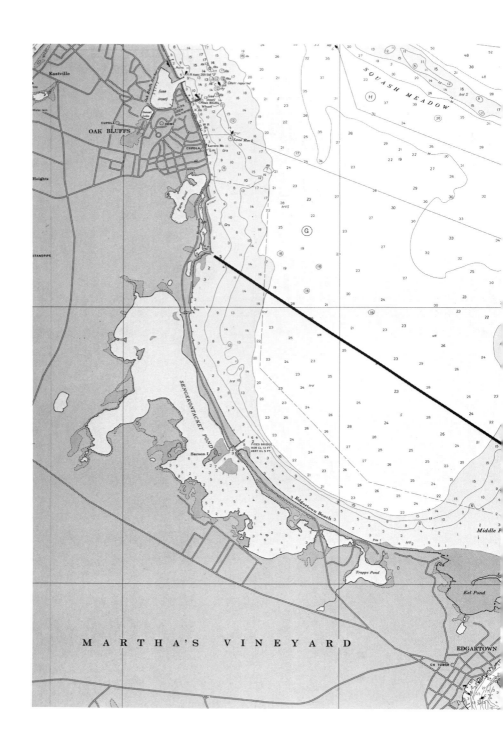

to be no more than 40 feet across, to find a protected harbor and a place where you can camp. Cape Poge Bay, though shallow, is about two miles long, north to south, a perfect place in which to sail your centerboarder. Best of all, near the lighthouse is a tiny natural harbor. It is guarded by an entrance two feet deep at dead low tide. There, even if you run aground, you can easily pull your boat off the sand, into slightly deeper water, and proceed.

What about the five-mile sail to Cape Poge Gut? You draw a line from the mouth of your harbor to buoy R "6", off the gut. Sailing this course you will pass across a place called Middle Flat, where there are rocks that are less than four feet below the surface at low tide. One isolated rock near your course is marked three feet.

Since these are tidal waters, you had better leave your harbor on an ebb and enter Cape Poge Gut on a flood. You consult your tide tables and discover that high tides at your harbor and at Cape Poge Gut occur at roughly the same time. A quick look at current tables tells you that in open water near your course there is little horizontal movement of the water.

Your plans will depend on the direction and the strength of the wind. In good weather, in this part of Massachusetts, the prevailing wind is southeast. In such a wind, you can sail more or less on a beam reach to and from your destination.

You are equipped with all the things you always carry when you sail, as well as a small tent, a sleeping bag, and a two-burner camping stove. You know it is possible to do without ice, but you want a hearty breakfast — orange juice, eggs, and bacon — so you buy a small ice chest in which to store these things.

The day before you plan to leave, the forecast is favorable. High tide will come at 10:00 A.M. You decide to leave at 11:00 A.M., and spend five hours sailing in the waters off the east coast of the Vineyard, having lunch aboard your boat, and approach Cape Poge Gut shortly after four o'clock, as the tide begins to flood. Once inside Cape Poge Bay, you can explore the place before you beach your boat and set up camp.

That night you stare again at Cape Poge Light. You tell yourself that your excitement is a little foolish. After all, you plan to sail a scant six miles. Even so, you anticipate the venture with a mixture of anxiety and pleasure.

In the morning, you depart, sailing through a narrow cut between two stone breakwaters. Overhead, the sky is blue. The wind is light, and as predicted, coming out of the southwest. The course you have marked on your chart, which ends at buoy R "6", takes you toward low, sandy land. Between you and the land is the buoy, but you can't see it yet. Your tide table told you that the drop from high to low tide at Cape Poge is slightly more than two feet, so it will indeed be safe to sail your intended course — a compass course of 140° magnetic.

As yet, you see no landmark or seamark near your course, so you sail by wind and compass. At first, the water is light green. Crossing some transparent shallows, you see a school of fish — small gray shadows darting, streaking, making shadows of their own. A single gull follows you, sunlight on her gray wing feathers.

Soon you are a mile from land. There are other boats abroad, but all are far away from you. Because you have learned to sail and have gained some confidence, you like the expanse of water, and the silence it provides.

As you approach Middle Flats, you consult your chart again. You can see the bottom clearly, sunlit sand shimmering, darkened here and there by grass. Since the water off your bow is reflecting midday light, tipping little waves with blue, you know you won't see a rock until you are just above it.

You sail swiftly, steadily across this crystal shallow ground. Suddenly, you see the dark shape of a rock on your right. Passing it, you sail into deeper water. You think you can see a buoy dead ahead, a speck against a line of dunes. R "6" marks the right-hand side of a channel leading past Edgartown and into Katama Bay, just south of Edgartown. You have time to make a detour, but as much as you would like to sail into Edgartown, you know that now, in a strong contrary current, you had better stay outside.

Sailing out of Edgartown is a racing boat whose picture you have seen in yachting magazines. Her sides are wet. Her decks are swarming with young sailors, setting a bright spinnaker. The 'chute ripples, red as flame, stabs the sky, pops and fills. You decide that you may set your spinnaker before the sailing season ends.

Just before five o'clock, you sail from a black can — C "7" — straight to Cape Poge Gut. You can see a rock marked on your chart on the right-hand side of the channel, so you hug the left-hand side. In the shelter of a bluff, the wind is weak and unpredictable. The current, stronger than you might have thought it would be at this time, takes you through the narrow cut. Inside, your centerboard strikes sand. As you raise it, the wind freshens and you enter Cape Poge Bay.

You sail into shallow reaches at the south end of the bay. Here, you see a lonely house whose windows, facing

A racing boat whose picture you may have seen in yachting magazines. (Bermuda News Bureau)

west, mirror glittering sunlight. As you sail, your centerboard touches bottom several times. You come about, and head directly toward the lighthouse.

As you enter the small natural harbor, you are running, so you raise your centerboard, skim across the sandy ridge, beach your boat, wade ashore, and set your anchor in the sand. You find a place to pitch your tent, set it up, and heat canned stew on your stove.

After supper, you traverse a nearby dune covered by the kinds of grasses which survive and flourish by the sea. You walk along a narrow beach. As you start back to your camp, the light of the setting sun warms the sand and touches flowers growing here — golden aster, clusters of rugosa rose.

Cape Poge light.

Excited, you wake up at dawn, leave your tent, and walk up a sandy road to the lighthouse. There you scan Nantucket Sound, looking east toward the sea. A fishing boat — a trawler several miles offshore, booms extended like a pair of ghostly arms — moves toward the fishing grounds. Now a sailing boat appears, heading east, outward bound. Knowing she may keep on sailing east, past Nantucket, into the Atlantic Ocean, it occurs to you that sailors can go almost anywhere. Their partnership with wind and water sets them free, as wings set free a migrant bird.

Moved by a strong impulse to sail again, you turn away. As you walk back toward your boat, you know that you have made a good beginning. Your pace quickens. By the time you have your breakfast, wash up, and strike your tent, the tide will have turned again and you can sail through Cape Poge Gut, on an ebb. Suddenly, you realize that you are thinking as a sailor thinks, that in fact you have become a sailor. In the east the sun is bright above a line of dappled cloud, signaling good times ahead, fair winds and sunny skies.

Part 3

Learning the Ropes

Three steps in tying a bowline, which is called the king of knots. The bowline makes a loop at the end of a line that is secure yet easy to untie. Make a loop as shown, pass the end of the line through the loop, around the line, and then back through the loop.

Basic Knots

It seems unfair to entice you to begin to learn to sail, promising bright days of sport, and then tell you you must first learn to tie at least five knots and tie them well. But if you want to sail, you must do this. Without several basic knots, you can't call yourself a sailor.

Sailing on the Charles River, Boston.

It won't be long before you set your spinnaker.

Sailmaker Peter Conrad at the helm of **Artemis***. Bill Tripp checks sail trim.*

Beam reaching. Mal and Betsy making furrows.

Sailing past two old-timers at Mystic Seaport, the whaling bark Charles W. Morgan *and the* Joseph Conrad.

Treat the sails with loving care.

Spinnaker trouble. If you have a spinnaker, leave it in its bag until you have mastered sailing under main and working jib.

Laser owners rigging boats for frostbiting.

Catboat racing in Buzzards Bay.

A brisk fall sail. Madison, Connecticut.

Blue Jays and lasers frostbiting on the Connecticut River at Essex.

IALA BUOYAGE SYSTEM

Lateral Aids marking the sides of channels seen when entering from Seaward.

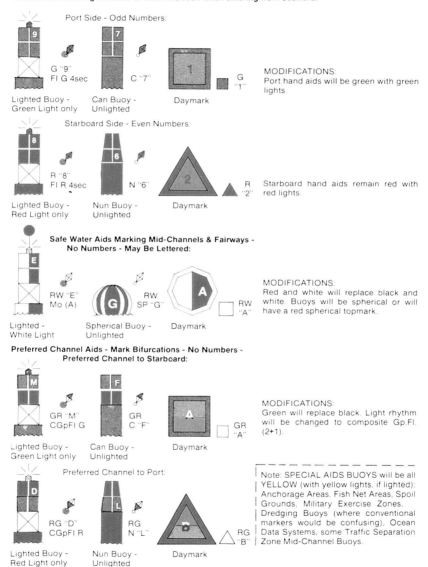

Port Side - Odd Numbers:

G "9"
Fl G 4sec

Lighted Buoy -
Green Light only

C "7"

Can Buoy -
Unlighted

Daymark

G "1"

MODIFICATIONS:
Port hand aids will be green with green lights.

Starboard Side - Even Numbers:

R "8"
Fl R 4sec

Lighted Buoy -
Red Light only

N "6"

Nun Buoy -
Unlighted

Daymark

R "2"

Starboard hand aids remain red with red lights.

Safe Water Aids Marking Mid-Channels & Fairways -
No Numbers - May Be Lettered:

RW "E"
Mo (A)

Lighted -
White Light

RW
SP "G"

Spherical Buoy -
Unlighted

Daymark

RW "A"

MODIFICATIONS:
Red and white will replace black and white. Buoys will be spherical or will have a red spherical topmark.

Preferred Channel Aids - Mark Bifurcations - No Numbers -
Preferred Channel to Starboard:

GR "M"
CGpFl G

Lighted Buoy -
Green Light only

GR
C "F"

Can Buoy -
Unlighted

Daymark

GR "A"

MODIFICATIONS:
Green will replace black. Light rhythm will be changed to composite Gp.Fl. (2+1).

Preferred Channel to Port:

RG "D"
CGpFl R

Lighted Buoy -
Red Light only

RG
N "L"

Nun Buoy -
Unlighted

Daymark

RG "B"

Note: SPECIAL AIDS BUOYS will be all YELLOW (with yellow lights, if lighted): Anchorage Areas, Fish Net Areas, Spoil Grounds, Military Exercise Zones, Dredging Buoys (where conventional markers would be confusing), Ocean Data Systems, some Traffic Separation Zone Mid-Channel Buoys.

Courtesy Eldridge Tide and Pilot Book.

I have known several people who seemed smart and capable until they tried to learn to tie a knot. One friend of mine, faced with an impatient teacher, walked away, giving up altogether. Others fumbled endlessly.

I urge you not to learn to tie knots on a boat, under stress. You can learn best tying them alone, around your leg or a bedpost. All you need is a length of supple rope, maybe four or five feet long, and clear photographs or drawings of the knots you want to learn, with brief captions under them.

I learned to tie sailors' knots after I bought my first boat in the fall. Looking forward to a launching on May 1, I stocked up on books on sailing. One of these was about marlin spike seamanship, which is the art of doing almost anything conceivable with rope — tying knots, *whipping, splicing,* making *monkey's fists,* etc.

I read some books, including several sailing stories which evoked storms at sea and heroic wanderings. The book on knots gathered dust.

At last, I was sick and spent a day or so in bed. On my blanket lay a length of nylon rope. Even so, I was reluctant to proceed. I thought I might grow bored with

Reef knot, or square knot. This common knot has few uses in a boat or on a dock. With this type of knot you can join the ends of two lines, but once the knot has been pulled tight, it can't easily be untied.

A lazy eight is a knot often used on the end of a line, to keep it from running through a block.

Tying a half-hitch (left); and the finished knot (right).

Another view of two half-hitches. A half-hitch has uses similar to a clove hitch but is less likely to become untied or slip.

Clove hitch.

Another view of a clove hitch, a good knot to use when securing a line to a piling or a stanchion.

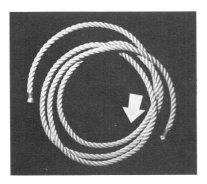

Most lines used in small boats are made so that they must be coiled clockwise or they will kink.

How to coil and make up a line when it is not in use: with your eye, simply undo what was done here. Now you can do it up again.

learning how to tie a hitch or two, a figure-eight, and what some people call the king of knots — a bowline.

Once I started, however, I was pleasantly surprised. I found that learning to tie knots was diverting and rewarding, and this knowledge, once acquired and practiced, stayed with me.

Do what I did. Learn these knots. You will need and tie them often.

Rules of the Road

However small your boat may be, sail away knowing basic rules of navigation which apply to daytime sailing. These rules were of course formulated simply to avoid collisions.

It is not realistic to expect a small-boat skipper to set sail equipped with running lights and riding lights. All you need to survive an unexpected sail in darkness is a little common sense. If you are caught after dark, stay away from shipping lanes and shine a spotlight on your sail now and then, especially when you see or hear a boat approaching.

When you start to pilot sailboats under power and become a nightime sailor, study the rules of the road in a book called *Chapman: Piloting, Seamanship, & Small Boat Handling.**

I have chosen to include two photographic diagrams showing things which are hard to describe. In general, any small boat should keep out of the way of a large boat or ship if possible, especially in a narrow channel. A sailboat close-hauled has the right of way over boats on other points of sailing. A boat running must maneuver to avoid boats on other points of sailing. If two boats sailing close-hauled are on a collision course, the boat on the starboard tack has the right of way over the boat on the port tack. This is why, when racing boats are at the starting line, you sometimes hear a skipper calling, "Starboard! Starboard!"

For two boats running, much the same rule applies. A boat running on a port jibe must avoid one running on a starboard jibe. In order to remember this without use of sailing language, bear in mind that your boat almost always has the right of way when you are sailing with the wind on your right hand.

---

* Chapman, Charles F. *Piloting, Seamanship, & Small Boat Handling*, published by *Motor Boating*, is called by some the boatman's bible. It is updated and republished often.

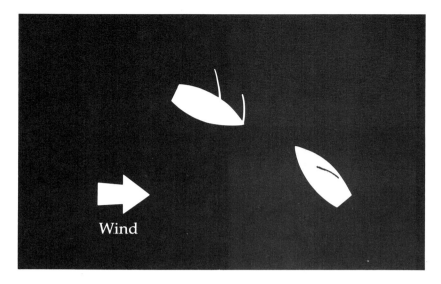

A boat sailing close-hauled has the right of way. Any boat with the wind abeam has the right of way over a boat on a broad reach or run.

Boats sailing more or less in one direction on the same tack may not be sailing a parallel course. If their courses are converging, the skipper in the boat to windward is presumed to have better control of his boat and therefore must change course to avoid the other boat.

Any boat approaching any other boat from a direction *abaft* — to the rear of — the port or starboard beam is said to be an overtaking boat and must avoid the boat it is gaining on. In other words, if you are coming up behind someone, you must bear responsibility for avoiding a collision.

There exists a kind of undeclared war between sailing skippers and the captains of small powerboats. Some sailors wave at other sailors passing and refuse to wave

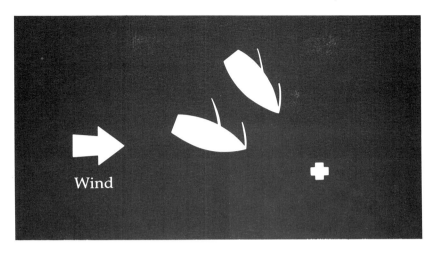

Here, the leeward boat has the right of way.

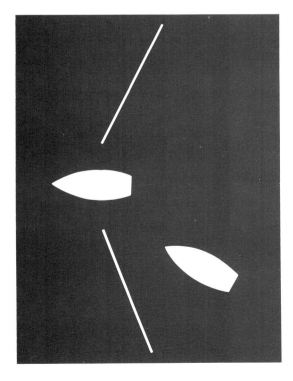

In zone designated here, the lead boat has the right of way over the overtaking boat.

at powerboats. Good skippers, whether under sail or power, scorn this kind of snobbery. A good powerboat captain understands the uses of the wind as well as many sailors do and can often execute maneuvers under power with more skill. There are skippers of both sail and powerboats, who are less than competent. Since you are a small-boat sailor without any power, play it safe: Don't expect your fellow boatmen to know all the rules, especially a sailor's rules.

On a recent fall day, I was sailing in a stiff wind in Nantucket Sound. One other boat was visible, a giant trawler dragging massive fishing nets. By the time I saw the ship and had identified her, there was very little time to maneuver to avoid her and her nets. My small boat was at the mercy of this monster. The trawler's captain knew that sailboats have the right of way over boats under power. He changed course to avoid me. Had he been ignorant, I might well have found myself enmeshed in the fringes of his nets, at the mercy of the sea.

Because a sailboat under sail is slower, and in general not as easy to maneuver as a boat under power, know your rights and enjoy them, but give way when necessary.

Navigation

Navigation, simply stated, is the practice of directing any craft from one position to another. Master navigators use not only scientific knowledge but accumulated judgment. In the sense that art is ingenuity in adapting natural things to man's use, navigation is an art.

You will start with what is called *piloting,* a set of skills that can be learned and sharpened without vast experience. At first, use simple, inexpensive instruments — one or two compasses, a chart and some current tables if you need them, a set of *parallel rules,* a *protractor,* a pair of *dividers,* a pad, several pencils, and a soft eraser. Although your computations will be easy, you might also use a calculator.

So far, you have sailed close to home, close to shore, and under optimum conditions, with blue skies, warm weather, light winds, and weak currents. You've had a chart and could read some of its signs, but though you may have had a compass, your eyes were your instruments. You saw landmarks and seamarks that you could use as reference points. So far, if you have had a compass, you have given little thought to it. Now, with long-range goals as well as present needs in mind, learn to use one as you should. Learn to use two, one mounted on the boat you sail, and the other carried on a string around your neck — a hand-bearing compass.

All small-boat compasses contain what are called compass cards — often thin aluminum discs marked off in degrees — which are suspended in a fluid in which they revolve freely. Underneath the card, guiding it, is a pair of *bar magnets,* each of which has a north-seeking end. These bar magnets are arranged so as to pull the point marked north — a letter "N" or figure zero — toward a point in the Earth's magnetic field. Toward what point?

As if it had a magnet near its center, Earth attracts other magnets but its forces are distributed unevenly. As a result, in most places, the north-seeking end of a bar magnet, like those found in compasses, seldom points

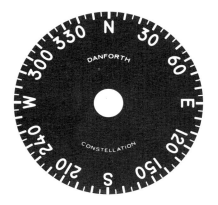

A compass card of the type used on a small boat. (Danforth compass card, Rule Industries)

toward *true north*, the geographic place you see marked on globes. Neither does it often point toward the north magnetic pole — a place 900 miles or so from the geographic pole. It isn't necessary here to explain the complex action of the Earth's attractions, but I will tell you how to use them.

According to a compass's location on the surface of the Earth, it tells you altogether different stories. As you sail, let's say from the English Channel to the Bay of Biscay or from Florida to Maine, the north-seeking end of your bar magnet points to various locations; but with very few exceptions, it will point toward the same place when you sail in one location. I will tell you more about this as you learn to use your compass in conjunction with a chart.

In most compasses, the compass card is marked off at every five degrees. Some have letters indicating directions, NE for northeast, and so on. As I noted earlier, the four primary compass points are marked N, E, S, W, and/or 0, 90, 180, 270. You can understand the marks on any compass if you study them awhile.

In "A Quick Look at Chart and Compass" (page 24), I said very little about the compass you have mounted or will mount on the boat you sail. If the boat has a compass, make sure it is working properly. If you buy one, pick a style that suits your boat. There are many kinds of compass mounts — bracket mounts, flush mounts, yoke mounts, and, on larger boats, binnacle mounts. On boats like the kinds I've recommended for beginning sailors, you will most likely find a bracket mount.

In some cases, installation may be easy, but in others you may have to have it done by someone who has had some experience. Before you buy, make sure the compass's internal compensators have been *zeroed in,* which simply means that they will have no effect on the working of the compass.

Three types of compass mounts: bracket mount (left), flush mount (center), and bulkhead mount (right). (Corsair II compasses, Rule Industries)

Before you go to work, read the instruction folder that came with your compass and check your pockets to make sure they don't contain things that might affect the operation of the compass. A wristwatch, a stopwatch, or a camera might cause problems. Loose objects can be tested easily. When you put them near the compass, you will see the compass card move. Don't drill holes in your boat until you know exactly where you want the compass.

Sit down aboard your boat in positions you will be in when you steer, on both port and starboard tacks. Mount your compass in a place where you can read it easily. Put it as far away as possible from where you have stored your anchor, chain, and things containing batteries — flashlights, calculators, and radios. Brass, aluminum and sometimes stainless steel are safe. Iron, steel, and lead are not.

Before you mount the compass, move it slowly and carefully around your boat, keeping its *lubber's lines* — the vertical line in a compass from which readings can be made — on or parallel to the boat's center line. If it behaves erratically, it is responding to magnetic influences other than the ones you want it to respond to. On a small boat, with no engine, you will probably not have large batteries or wires through which current flows, but as I say, small batteries can cause disasters. Back in 1956, in a race, William F. Buckley, aboard his boat *Panic,* landed on a stack of rocks one night when his compass failed him. A small flashlight battery stowed near the *Panic*'s compass had put Buckley 11° off his intended course. Things like this happen to the best of skippers.

Mount your compass on your boat's centerline or on

a line exactly parallel to it. The compass should be level in order to reduce the effect of the boat's motion. Mount the compass using nonmagnetic screws or nuts and bolts. These and a small brass screwdriver — for use in adjusting compensators — often come with compasses. Drill the holes for bolts carefully, using a small pilot hole. For screws, use a pilot hole.

Now learn to use the compass in conjunction with your chart. As you read this, you must have a chart beside you. As you have seen, using scales on a chart, you can find the distances between two points, in statute miles (the kind we use on land), in nautical miles, kilometers, yards, or meters. If you can guess at your boat's speed, you can figure roughly how long it will take you to sail between the two points.

Draw a light pencil line from where your boat is moored or docked to your objective. Is your course clear of other people's moorings, clear of islands, rocks, shoals, and other hazards? If it is, and you can sail to it without tacking, you have drawn what can become your compass course.

The link between your chart and compass is a compass rose. There may be one set of these or two or more on your chart. Pick the set nearest to the course you've marked. As I said earlier, a set consists of two, sometimes three, separate circles, one or two inside the larger or the largest. The outer one indicates *true north* and its attendant points, marked in degrees. The next circle is one you may have used before. It indicates magnetic north and its attendant points. This compass rose is valid only in the region which surrounds it, in the year the chart was issued. If your chart has a third compass rose inside

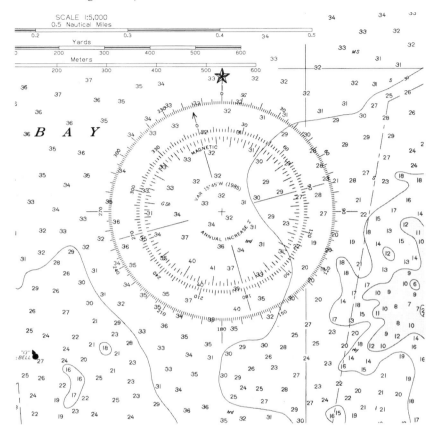

This is a compass rose of a kind found on most charts and described in the text.

the other two, ignore it. Marked out in a different way — one point equalling 11° 15′ — it will only make an easy job more difficult.

Earlier, I suggested that you use only one compass rose, the one indicating magnetic north. Now, as you learn to navigate, eliminate this shortcut and begin to use the compass rose that indicates true north, and add or subtract the stated *variation*, which is found inside the inner compass rose. Variation is the difference in degrees between true north and magnetic north, the place your compass points to as it is affected by the particular magnetic forces in the region where you sail. More about this as you learn to *lay a course* — learn to plot it on your chart.

Place the outer edge of one of your parallel rules along the pencil course you have drawn on your chart. Walk or slide the rules across the chart, one at a time, toward the nearest compass rose. Never let both rules move at the same time. Keep them exactly parallel to the

Chart, parallel rules, and divider.

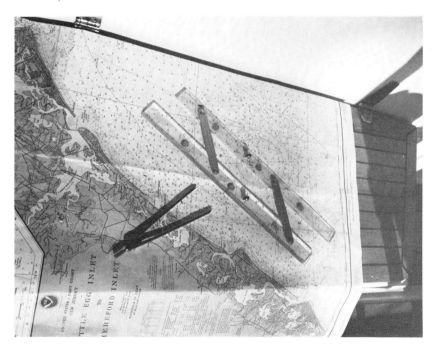

pencil line you've drawn. When one of them passes through the center of the compass rose you are using, read your heading on the outer circle. Let's say your true course turns out to be 22°. If the variation noted in the compass rose is VAR 14° E — meaning east — *subtract* 14 from 22. The answer, 8°, is your magnetic heading, the one you will sail using your compass or your compasses. If the variation is marked W — or west — the same number of degrees, *add* 14 to 22. Remember when the compass course indicates a course to the right of your true course, the variation is east, and when it indicates a course to the left, it is west. When the variation is west, add it to your true course to determine your magnetic course. When the variation is east, subtract it from your true course.

If as you sail you have reason to suspect that your compass isn't working properly, you can do a rough check by sailing between two points directly north and south of one another and sail back, then sailing between two other points directly east and west of each other and return. On both courses, if the compass indicates correctly the direction in which you are sailing, it is working as it should.

Now that you know how to find a magnetic heading and to sail it, with the compass which is mounted on your boat, why use a hand-bearing compass? For one thing, because you can hold it in your hand and move it freely. Using its vanes, which resemble sights on a gun barrel, you can take *bearings* with it — that is, you can locate things around you in relation to your boat, in terms of direction. See that steeple over there? It is northwest of your boat. Then its bearing is northwest.

There are several ways to use a hand-bearing compass. Let us suppose that you are sailing in a vast expanse of water but can see several landmarks and seamarks. The compass mounted on your boat indicates magnetic north. You know your course but you don't know your position. This time, instead of guessing as you did before, you want an accurate position. Maybe you must skirt a shoal or avoid a pile of rocks.

Aiming your hand-bearing compass at a landmark or seamark that appears on your chart, take bearing number one, and read it on the compass card. Draw a line on your chart, from the landmark or seamark, which extends beyond your position, which has not yet been determined. You are someplace on this line which is called a *line of position.* Now take a second bearing. This

Determine your position using a hand-bearing compass.

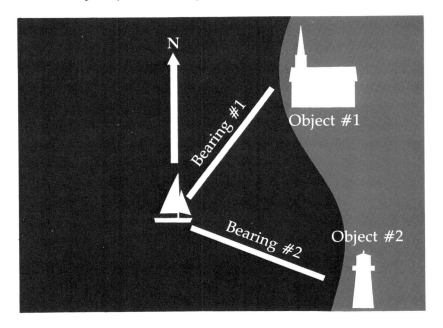

time aim at something else, if possible an object 45° or more from the first landmark or seamark. Draw a line indicating bearing number two, extending it past the point where the lines cross. The point where they cross is your position.

You will find other uses for your hand-bearing compass. For example, by sighting periodically a boat sailing toward you, you can determine if you and the other boat are on a collision course. If the bearing of the boat approaching stays the same, one of you must change course.

You may not use all this knowledge right away, but I predict that soon you will want more information and will turn to books on piloting and navigation which are more advanced than this one.

It is fun to navigate, especially when things work out well. Once, when I was with him, *Blixtar*'s skipper, Danny Miller, used dead reckoning to sail from a point off Bermuda to Montauk Light on Long Island. We approached the coast in fog and suddenly we saw the light, rising up above the mist. After an extended voyage, Danny was right on target.

Notes on Currents

Currents are a horizontal movement of a mass of water. Tides — caused by the attraction of the sun and moon — are the alternate rising and falling of the surface of the ocean and the bays, gulfs, sounds, and lower reaches of rivers connected to the ocean.

In large bodies of water, *tidal currents* — currents

caused by tidal action — are not strong, but when an ebbing or a flooding tide causes water to run through a narrow place, they can be strong enough to sweep your small boat with them so you cannot sail at all. For example, in a narrow river gorge, there are rapids. In a harbor where you sail, currents may be very weak, almost indiscernible, until you approach the harbor's mouth, where you may encounter currents that will carry your boat out to sea, or backward, making it impossible for you to escape the harbor. Tides go from low to high or high to low in slightly more than six hours, which means that the time lapse between two high tides or two low tides is more than twelve hours. As tidal currents turn — go from one direction to another — they are weak. In the middle of a flood, they are strong, as they are in the middle of an ebb. You will see these things noted on current tables.

Since tides are predictable, tidal currents can be forecast. Using tide and current tables, mariners can predict the speed of currents in California's Golden Gate or in the Narrows in New York, at, say, 3:00 P.M. on September 25 of any year.

When you want to learn to sail in strong currents, using them to your advantage, you will learn to use these tables. I will tell you where to buy them in "Charts and Tide and Current Tables," on page 134.

As I suggested earlier, because you sail in a light boat, without an engine, it is best to keep away from all but the weakest currents.

Even so, you must know how currents will influence you as you lay a course and sail it. In some places, river currents always flow downstream, but as they approach a river's mouth emptying into tidal waters, tides affect them and for several hours at a time, on a flood, they can flow upstream. Of course, conversely, on an ebb their speed is magnified.

Now, using an example, I will tell you how to sail from point A to point B across a current. You plan to cross a wide river or a tidal channel, sailing toward a little town one mile away. The currents are quite strong, flowing south. They are stronger in the middle of the channel than along the banks, in coves, and other partly sheltered places. Let's say the current averages 2 miles an hour. You are smart enough to know that if you aim straight at the town and continue to do so, you will drift in a southerly direction and will never reach the town. When you finish your frustrating voyage, you will be downcurrent someplace, on the shore opposite, with your bow pointing toward the town, and your magnetic compass heading will have changed, maybe by as much as 45°.

Let's say your average speed is 4 miles an hour. In slack water, you could sail straight to the town in a quarter of an hour, while in a 2-mile-an-hour current, you will drift downstream half a mile in a quarter of an hour. This indicates that you must draw a line on your chart before you sail, from your point of departure toward a point at least a half-mile north of the town, note the magnetic heading indicated by it, and keep sailing on that heading as you cross. The line you've drawn on your chart is not your course. You won't sail along this line. In plotting it, you were simply figuring what magnetic heading you will sail in order to correct for drift.

You can translate this example into slightly more complex calculations and determine any compass course across water which is moving more or less at right angles to your course. To do so, you have to know only the average speed of the movement of the water and, of course, your boat's speed. If you sail on a river, at a point not near its mouth, you will sail with local knowledge and will know about how fast the waters of the river move. As I say, if you live in tidal waters, you can learn about the currents using tide and current tables.

Violent Storms

NOAA weather forecasts predict wind speeds and wave heights, and tell you times of high and low tides. They tell you when you may expect strong winds and violent storms — squall lines, hurricanes, typhoons, and tornadoes. Weather experts spot squall lines and plot their paths. If one is approaching you, secure your boat and stay on land. Hurricanes and typhoons are always forecast in advance, and you can prepare for them. In spring and summer in some regions, lake sailors should be alert for the appearance of tornadoes. These violent whirls, the most destructive storms in the Earth's atmosphere, are heralded by the sight of funnels forming near a cloud base, growing downward. They are often heralded by abrupt wind shifts, sudden dampness, and/or sharp drops in temperature.

If scattered thunderstorms are in your neighborhood, stay at home. If you are on the water when a thunderstorm appears, you won't have much time for play. You might sail to a sheltered place and anchor, but if the storm seems far away, you may have time to sail back home. Figure out how far away it is, then decide what to do. When you see a flash of lightning, with your stopwatch note the number of seconds that pass between the flash and the sound of thunder. Divide by five and you will know how far away, in miles, the storm is.

Thunderstorms along a systematic squall line often indicate the arrival of a cold front and are more predictable. They are deadly, sometimes bringing winds of one hundred miles an hour. Squall lines are preceded by incessant lightning and enormous cloud formations that are dark and puffy on their undersides.

One afternoon, I encountered a squall line, or a storm that was part of a squall line. I was sailing with a

When cottony, fair weather clouds begin to build into vertical heaps, they often signal thunderstorms, which can bring high winds, lightning, rain, and hail. (Photo courtesy N. S. Wilson)

friend near Stonington, Connecticut. Winds were light. A sultry haze hung above the land and water. My mate and I were hypnotized by the silence and the heat. We failed to notice that the sky was growing dark. Clouds were climbing ever higher. As the wind began to shift, my mate became concerned. "What's happening?"

The air grew cool. The wind picked up alarmingly. Thunderheads swept across the gray-green sky. We didn't know it then, but we were looking at what is called a mammatus sky. Whitecaps danced all around us. When I tried to sail to windward, I saw that I had lost control. By then the boat was rolling, pitching violently. My mate suggested that we'd better douse the sails. This, of course, was good advice. We should have done it as the storm bore down on us, before the boat began to do its violent dance. Skidding on the heaving foredeck, I took off the jib while my mate brought down the mainsail, and at last we dropped our anchor, and rode out the storm.

Back home, we found out that the winds had indeed been very strong, blowing fifty knots in gusts. In fact, the squall line had caused problems for a lot of seasoned skippers. Several boats had been dismasted not far from our anchorage.

Cold and Fog

Violent storms and strong currents are not the only sailing hazards. Cold water is a killer. Fog can be a sudden menace.

As you learn to sail your boat, the water temperature should be at least 60° Fahrenheit. During World War II,

In winter clothing, Blue Jay sailors getting ready for frostbiting in Essex, Connecticut.

many sailors wearing winter clothing and life jackets perished almost instantly in northern seas. In higher water temperatures, swimmers last a little longer.

Fog can move in very fast, blanketing the sea and land. Parts of the states of Washington, California, and Maine are noted for their fogs, but fogs appear in other places. I have been a victim of obliterating fogs in Fishers Island Sound and on San Francisco Bay. Unless you have a battery of sophisticated instruments, there is only one good way to sail in fog. Once you see it coming, spot a place you want to sail to and, using a compass, sail the necessary course. As you go, blow your foghorn frequently and remember that a fog distorts all sounds, or seems to. Never follow a foghorn. Give a fixed horn a wide berth. In most cases, it marks rocks. If you see a floating buoy, resist the urge to cling to it. Small boats, any boats, tied to buoys make the buoys harder to identify, and this endangers other ships and boats. Use the buoy as an aid to navigation. Note its shape and its color. Read its number. Find it on your chart and, with your compass, sail a course toward your objective.

Good weather, dominated by a high pressure system, brings brisk winds, azure skies, and small white clouds, floating tufts called *cumulus clouds.* You will learn to know good sailing weather when you see it. As you begin, sail only on light-air days — when the wind is not too strong. As you learn, you will sail with confidence.

Equip Your Boat and Yourself

Small as she is, your boat should be equipped with things that will make sailing safer and more fun. Give attention to the boat, her equipment, and your clothing.

There was a time when a hand-bearing compass, a spotlight, and other useful and/or necessary things were heavy and expensive, when they were sinkable and might have seemed to have no place aboard a small boat. Now plastic compasses, light waterproof spotlights that float if they fall overboard, and other nautical equipment can be bought for very little money and will not encumber you. The list below includes suggestions. If you can't buy all the things on the list, buy the necessary ones and wait until you can afford the others. You won't always carry everything you own, especially if you race your boat, but

the sooner you can own and learn to use things like these
the sooner you will build the kind of confidence that will
put you in command of yourself, your boat, your crew.

General Equipment
Anchor, chain, and anchor rode
Boat hook
Boom crutch
Bucket with a length of line attached to its handle
Docking lines and a tow line
Fenders
First aid kit in waterproof container
Flashlight or spotlight, waterproof and floatable
Horn

Anchor, paddle, and boom crutch.

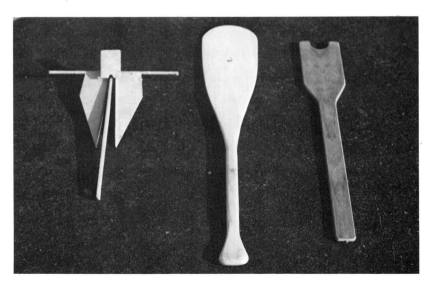

Navigation Equipment

Calculator

Chart or charts

Compass mounted on the boat

Dividers

Hand-bearing compass

Hand-held speedometer

Pad, pencil, eraser

Parallel rules

Protractor

Stopwatch, on a string or leather thong

Tide and current tables

VHF weather radio

Underneath the hand-held yachting speedometer are (clockwise): hand-bearing compass, boat compass, stopwatch, and VHF radio.

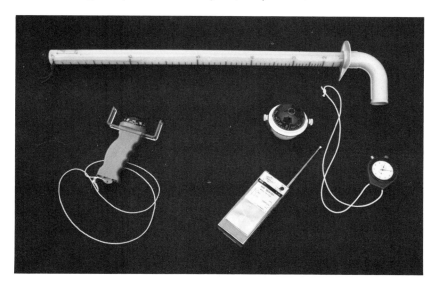

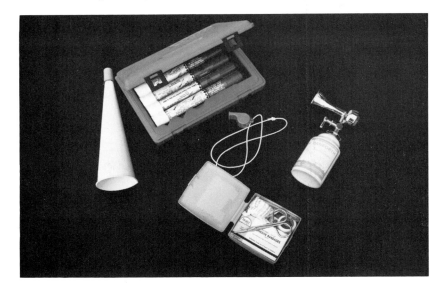

Surrounding the whistle with a lanyard attached are (clockwise): a mouth horn, a flag and flare kit, a Danforth horn, and a small first aid kit. Both flare and first aid kits are in waterproof containers.

Emergency and Safety Equipment

Flag and flare kit

Life jackets with whistles tied to them for skipper and crew members, and at least one spare life jacket and some floatable cushions

Paddle or paddles

Spare tiller

Tools and spare parts, things like shackles, cotter pins, and nuts and bolts

Long ago, on a bright day, I sailed a boat of mine with a friend to an island several miles from my home port. My mate was a hardy Englishman, who had sailed in the North Sea. When he brought a sweater and foul weather jacket with him, I thought he was being much too cautious. I was careless. I wore shorts and a light cotton shirt. As we sailed home, the sky turned gray. The temperature must have dropped ten degrees. My friend put on his sweater right away. The wind picked up and the spray began to fly across our bow. My friend put on his jacket. In my wet shirt, I grew cold. My teeth chattered. I could scarcely hold the tiller, so my friend sailed us home, while I retreated to the cabin shivering.

Later on, I learned to protect myself from the wet and the cold. I suggest you do the same. If you do, you will celebrate the sport while friends of yours stay at home.

In warm weather, you will see a lot of sailors carrying sweaters, knowing that the warmest days can cool and chill you as the sun sets. Even in the mildest weather, most sailors carry light waterproof jackets; because without a jacket, even on a light-air day, you can soak your clothing through. Keep your clothes and your skin as dry as possible.

Malcolm Nicholls, reading my advice to you, reminded me that it is impossible to stay dry in a small boat, and he suggested woolen clothing — trousers, sweaters, even hats — on a cold day, because wool is warmer even after a good soaking than most other fabrics are. I have found that cotton T-shirts next to my skin help when I wear them under wool. Malcolm also recommends that you avoid bulky clothing, which will catch on things as you move around a boat.

As you can see in many pictures in this book, Malcolm wears sailing gloves, not for warmth, but to keep his hands from blistering as he works with sheets and halyards. He recommends buying and wearing a wetsuit in chilly weather, if you can afford to buy one, though he emphasizes that they are expensive and for fair weather sailing aren't necessary.

Tips on Trailing

Many boats are trailable. If you decide to buy a boat, it may come with a trailer. If not, buy one if you can.

With a trailer, you can haul your boat, lay it up in wintertime, and launch it in the spring. It will extend your sailing range.

When I took the photographs for this book, I trailed a Blue Jay many miles, in company with two young sailors. We launched the boat at Mystic Seaport, where we did some river sailing in that fascinating place. We took the boat to other harbors, sailed in Fishers Island Sound and Little Narragansett Bay. Had we had the inclination, we might well have gone to farflung lakes and bays. If you decide to race your boat, you can trail her to regattas miles from home.

Your trailer must suit your boat. Make sure your trailer hitch is a good one, properly installed with bolts, lock-washers, and nuts. Make sure its coupling ball is the right size. Remember to attach the safety chains. Feed the hooks in from the underside — up through the holes, not down into them.

Your boat is at home in the water, not on land. Be sure to make her comfortable, seeing that her hull has soft support. Equip yourself with lengths of line and, using bowlines, hitches, and whatever other knots you need, tie the boat to the trailer so it won't slide off its cradle. Pad the ropes where they pass across the rail and other places where their constant chafing motion might do damage. Wrap or pad them where they pass around or over metal members of the trailer. These are often very sharp. On land as well as water, chafing can wear a rope straight through. With this in mind, stop now and then and check the ropes at points which are critical.

The mast must be secured so it won't move forward and impale your car or slide backward and fall off. Tie a red flag at the end that sticks out beyond the transom of your boat.

As you prepare, think what will happen when the trailer's little wheels go over bumps. Allow for jolts and the action of the wind against your hull. Never overload your boat. She can carry her own mast, boom, and sails, but little more. Never carry passengers in the boat.

Whoever drives must have experience in trailing or must practice in an empty lot. As he drives, he must be constantly aware of the trailer he is pulling, and remember, backing takes a lot of practice.

There are many launching ramps throughout the United States and in other countries too. You can use most of these without paying a service charge.

Attach a bow and stern line to the boat so you can guide it and maneuver it once it hits water. As you will when you are sailing, note which way the wind is blowing. Make a plan.

In most cases, you can simply back the trailer into the water, and move the boat back on the trailer's rubber rollers to a place where you can launch it. Of course, in launching, many hands do indeed make lighter work, and remember it is harder to reload than launch. Don't launch in a secluded place unless you're sure you can reload.

If your trailer is not equipped with brakes, carry wheel chocks — triangular blocks of wood to use to keep the wheels from rolling. You may need these during launches when the trailer stands alone on a grade.

If you have trailed your boat a long way, don't immerse the trailer's wheels until they cool. A sudden change in temperature creates a partial vacuum in the bearings, which will draw the water in. In time, this will destroy the bearings.

A Blue Jay on a trailer, rigged and ready to be launched.

While you wait, step the mast and rig the boat. Bend on the sails if you want to. Furl them carefully. Make sure all the ports are closed so your boat won't start to sink as soon as it is water-borne. At launch, keep a tight hold on the lines at bow and stern so your boat won't float away.

Before you sail or paddle off, roll the trailer off the ramp. In some places, it is safe to leave a trailer unattended, but in others it is not. Padlock it either to your car, or to a fence or pole.

By now, you know enough about the wind and points of sailing to know how to leave the ramp, but in an onshore wind, the best way may be to wade out into shallow water, climb aboard, and paddle out. If you do this with a mate, stay on one side while your mate stays on the other so that you can keep the rails from going under as you climb aboard.

When you sail back to the ramp, luff your sails and ghost up into shallow water. If the trailer is positioned properly, two young sailors using ropes can pull a small boat up and over to its cradle. Under difficult conditions, two adults may find they have to ask for help. On shore, do the things you did before, in reverse order.

If you *dry sail* — store your boat out of water — you may use a crane to launch her or a ramp that you will use repeatedly. If you launch in tidal waters, keep a tide table handy so that you can launch at times when both launching and reloading can be done conveniently.

If, during launches and reloadings, you have had to douse your trailer's wheels, especially in salt water, give attention to the bearings. If you want to keep them working, they should be repacked every time you submerge them. This can be done at any service station.

Salt water is a trailer's enemy. When you hose off your boat and sails, wash down your trailer, too. If you take care of your boat, its sails, and trailer, they will serve you many years, so you can trail and sail again.

Buying a Boat

Choose a boat for its sailing qualities. Ask yourself some telling questions. Does the boat handle easily? How well will it go to windward? Is it stable, so that you can sail it on a fairly windy day? Is it suitable for the waters where you want to sail? Is it a popular class of boat so that if you want to race it, you can test yourself against your fellow sailors?

There are beautiful small-keel boats. Good ones are expensive and are heavy, but are good sea boats, and if you live on coastal waters, they will give you greater range than you would have sailing a small centerboarder. As you become a sailor, as you learn about the tides and currents, you can take them anywhere. In general, though, beginners prefer centerboards.

If you plan to trail your boat behind a car, look at ones that are light. Your boat should have *full flotation*, which means when it capsizes it will swamp but stay afloat so that you can stay with it. A boat's rig must suit its hull. Well-designed boats are equipped with a *rig* — a mast and a set of sails — which will move the hull along efficiently but won't overpower it. In other words, hull and boat must work together perfectly.

Many people learn to sail in sailing dinghies — small boats which are suitable for both rowing and sailing. For example, Mystic Seaport has an excellent program in which they use Dyer Dhows, perhaps the best of sailing dinghies in construction and design. There, as in many schools, they employ a chase or crash boat, a powerboat used for rescue and instruction. This accompanies the dinghies, which capsize quite frequently. In a highly organized program, run by experts, sailing dinghies are acceptable, but there are better boats for beginners.

Sailboards, Sunfish, Lasers, Phantoms, and boats of similar design are great fun under optimum conditions, but only stronger sailors wearing wetsuits can extend their range and season and go out in windy weather.

Catboats are a good choice for shallow waters, and because they are wide, they are stable. However, though catboats only have one sail, in some ways a boat with a Marconi rig is easier to handle.

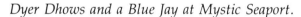

Dyer Dhows and a Blue Jay at Mystic Seaport.

In the lead.

The Styrofoam boats I have seen are dangerous. They bob like corks on the water. They have no authority. In such a boat a beginner can set out in a gusty offshore wind, run happily away from land, tack clumsily, and find that it's impossible to sail back home. My first encounter with a Styrofoam boat was my last. I took my daughter out in one in waters east of Martha's Vineyard. Shortly after we set sail, the wind picked up. When I saw how light the boat was, saw she wouldn't go to windward, I grew frightened. So, of course, did my daughter. We were lucky. When I hailed the skipper of a powerboat, he picked us up. Subsequently, I became a better sailor and made ocean passages, but I've never forgotten what I learned that day. A skipper is no better than his boat.

Whatever boat you plan to sail, there will surely come a time when you will covet other boats. Malcolm Nicholls, who appears in many sailing photographs in this book, is a Blue Jay sailor, but he dreams of expensive yachts, sailing yachts *and* power yachts. He reads yachting magazines and answers ads for boats for sale. In return, brokers send him information — leaflets, brochures, things like that. Not long ago, he wrote to an English broker. The yacht that had caught his eye was a whopping motor sailer — 130 feet L.O.A., costing $4,375,000.00.

Ten days later, Malcolm got a call from London. He soon gathered that the call was connected to a boat, a *big* boat, with ten staterooms, a saloon, and a commodious sundeck. He blushed when it began to dawn on

Big sister.

him that the broker thought that Malcolm Nicholls, age fourteen, was a multimillionaire who might really buy the boat.

So go dreams. Though Malcolm races his Blue Jay, he favors sailing just for fun, rather than in competition. He sometimes wins a race, but other sailors his age are much more competitive, some fiercely so. Still others are reflective people who don't ever race, who prefer to sail alone or with a friend, in company with sky and water, wind and sun.

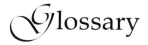lossary

Abaft. Toward the back of a boat.

About. To come or go about is to go from a close-hauled point of sailing to the opposite tack by swinging from a given course into the wind and a taking up a new course more or less at 90° to the old one.

Aft. Toward the back of a boat.

After. Behind or hindmost. For example, the after deck is behind the foredeck.

Anchor. A device that grips the bottom of a body of water.

Anchor rode. Anchor line.

Anemometer. An instrument that indicates wind speed.

Apparent wind. The direction from which the wind seems to be blowing when you are aboard a moving boat.

Astern. To the rear.

Backing the jib. Pushing the sail to windward so it will bring the bow around.

Backstay. Wire leading from the mast to the stern.

Bale. A metal loop on a mast, on which to shackle halyards not in use.

Batten pockets. Pockets in the leech of a sail which hold the battens.

Battens. Strips of wood or plastic used to stiffen the leech of a sail.

Beam. Width of boat.

Beam reach. A point of sailing on which the wind is coming at an angle of 90° to a boat's course.

Bearing. The direction of one object as related to another. For example, if a lighthouse is northwest of you, its bearing is northwest.

Beating. Sailing close-hauled toward a mark or an objective.

Before the wind. Having the wind coming from aft.

Bight. A simple loop. See photographic diagram, page 84.

Block. A pulley.

Boat hook. A pole with a hook at its end.

Boom. The spar to which the foot of a sail is attached.

Boom crutch. Usually a wooden crutch used to support the boom when the sail is not in use.

Boom tent. A canvas or plastic covering which fits over the boom and is tied to the sides of a boat.

Boom vang. A line reaching from a point on the boom to the mast near the deck. Used to help hold down the boom on a reach or a run and thus improve the trim of the mainsail.

Bow. The front or forward end of a boat.

Bow line. A docking line which goes from the bow of a boat to the dock.

Bowline. Sometimes called the king of knots. See photographic diagram, page 84.

Broach. To wing broadside to the wind.

Broad reach. A point of sailing between a beam reach and a run.

Buoy. An anchored floating object used as an aid to navigation.

Burgee. A small triangular yacht club flag.

Catspaws. Little ridges made by wind on the water, which take a parabolic shape.

Centerboard. A downward-pointing fin that can be adjusted so a boat will sail efficiently under various conditions.

Centerboard pendant or *pennant.* A line for raising and lowering the centerboard.

Chafe Guard. Usually a plastic tube around a mooring line or anchor line which protects it where it runs through a chock.

Chock. A fitting usually on the bow, designed to be a guide for a bow line, tow line, or anchor rode.

Cleat. A fitting used for securing halyards, sheets, and all lines which have to be adjusted as you sail. There are several kinds of cleats.

Clew. The lower after corner of a sail.

Close-hauled. When the sails are pulled in tight, and you are sailing as high as possible.

Close reach. A point of sailing between close-hauled and a beam reach.

Clove hitch. A good knot to use to secure a line to a piling. See photographic diagram, page 87.

Compass. A magnetic device that enables mariners to find magnetic north.

Compass card. In a compass, a disk marked out in degrees.

Compass rose. On a chart, a circle or circles marked out in degrees.

Deck. In general, anything aboard a boat you can step or walk on.

Dinghy. A small rowboat, sometimes called a pram, which is used to go short distances, usually to and from an anchorage or mooring. Some of these are sailing dinghies.

Dividers. Used mostly for measuring and comparing distances on a chart. If you have no dividers, mark off a piece of paper.

Double ended, or *double ender.* Any sailboat which is pointed at both ends.

Downhaul. A short line on the mast which is used to pull the boom and mainsail down slightly so as to tighten its luff.

Downwind. Sailing downwind is sailing more or less with the wind. The word also indicates a point to leeward.

Draft. The distance between water level and the bottom of a boat's centerboard or keel. If this distance is three feet, the boat is said to draw three feet. A centerboarder might draw three feet with centerboard down and one foot with it up.

Draw. See draft.

Dry sail. To store a boat on land instead of at a mooring or a dock.

Ease sheets. Let the sheets out but not let them go altogether. In general you should never let them go altogether.

Ebb tide. A receding tide.

Fall off. To steer away from the wind.

Fenders. Soft, enlongated objects which may be hung along the sides of a boat to protect it from a dock which itself has no fender.

Fetch. When you are sailing to windward and can make your mark without tacking.

Flood tide. A rising tide.

Foot. The bottom edge of a sail.

Fore. Ahead of.

Foredeck. The part of the deck forward of the mast.

Forestay. Wire leading from the masthead to the bow.

Foul weather gear. Waterproof clothing suitable for sailors.

Full floatation. A sailboat having air pockets that will keep it floating after it has capsized is said to have full floatation.

Furl. To roll or fold a sail up on a boom and secure it with stops.

Gate. A wide place in a slot in a mast or a break in a track provided so the fittings on the mainsail or a rope sewn into the luff of the mainsail can be introduced into the slot or track.

Genoa. A large jib which overlaps the mainsail.

Gooseneck fitting. The fitting which fastens the boom to the mast and allows the boom to swivel.

Halyards. Ropes, or lines, with which to raise the sails.

Hanked. Means *put.* "Put on the jib" is the same as "Hank on the jib." In most places in the text, I say "put," but remember what hank means.

Head. The topmost corner of a sail. Also a term for toilet.

Heel. The tilt of a boat under sail. A boat or ship which is tilting at a dock is said to be listing.

Helm. A tiller or wheel which directs the rudder.

High. To windward. In sailing, this term indicates a course in relation to the wind. For example, if you are sailing close-hauled, change your course and start to luff, you are too high to be sailing to advantage.

Hike out. To lean out to windward.

Hull. The main body of a boat.

Hull speed. The theoretical maximum speed of the hull before it begins to plow, to push its bow below the surface of the water.

Hull trim. If there is too much weight forward, aft, or on one side, the hull is poorly trimmed. The waterline, often painted on the board, suggests the proper trim.

In irons. When the bow is pointing more or less to windward and won't move off to either port or starboard tack.

Jib. A triangular sail set forward of the mast.

Jibe. A jibe occurs when sails and/or hull are maneuvered purposely or accidentally so that the wind comes around behind, filling the sail on the opposite side.

Keel. A fixed downward pointing fin, weighted at its bottom. The ballast at the bottom of a keel is often almost half the weight of the whole boat, keel included. This provides stability not found in a centerboard.

Knot. A unit of speed — one nautical mile per hour. A nautical mile is 6,080.20 feet, longer than a mile on land. A knot, therefore, is roughly 1.15 miles an hour. You will mark yourself as ignorant if you say knots per hour.

Laying a course. Plotting a course on a chart.

Lazy eight. A knot for the end of a line, to keep it from running through a block, an eye, or a gap. See page 86.

Lee. The side of an object sheltered from the wind.

Leech. The trailing edge of a sail.

Lee shore. A lee shore is one toward which the wind is blowing. In view of the above definition, this seems to make little sense. Just remember that the "lee shore" is exactly opposite to "in the lee of the shore."

Leeward. Away from the wind.

Lines. In general, ropes aboard a boat.

Line of position. A line drawn from a distant point to where you are. This can be an imaginary line or one drawn on a chart.

L.O.A. Length overall.

Lubber's line. A vertical line in a compass from which readings can be made.

Luff. The leading edge of a sail.

Luff, luffing. To spill wind, spilling wind. When you luff, the sail trembles, is not full.

L.W.L. Length at waterline.

Magnetic north. North as indicated by your compass in the place where you sail. This seldom coincides with true north.

Mainsail. Usually the largest sail. In a sloop like the Blue Jay, the sail whose luff is secured to the mast.

Marconi rig. A rig using tall triangular sails.

Mast. The vertical spar supporting the boom and sails.

Masthead. The top of a mast.

Masthead fly. A kind of weathervane on the masthead.

Money in the bank. When you are sailing toward a mark, proceeding past the point where you think you can fetch the mark.

Monkey's fist. A ball woven into the end of a line, which weights it so it can be heaved more easily.

Mooring. A permanent anchor on which to keep a boat.

Navigation. Determining a boat's position, using charts, instruments, and/or sun and stars, and with these means, directing it successfully from one point to another.

Off the wind. A number of degrees to leeward of the most efficient course. If you are off the wind but want to hold your course, ease your sheets.

Painter. A light line attached to the bow of a dinghy or any small boat, to tie the boat to a mooring or a dock.

Parallel rules. Two rules joined so that they are always parallel but may be separated and "walked" across a chart.

Pendant. Sometimes called a pennant. A mooring line, often with a loop at its end, or a short line used to raise and lower a centerboard.

Pennant. A small flag. Also called a pendant.

Piloting. Directing a boat in and out of a harbor or from one point to another, using visible landmarks, charts, tide and current tables, and instruments.

Pinching. Luffing slightly, moving sluggishly toward a mark or an objective, instead of tacking.

Port. Left-hand side. Also a harbor.

Porthole. Hole or window in a boat.

Port jibe. Running with the sail and boom on the starboard side.

Portside. Left-hand side.

Port tack. With the wind coming over the portside of a boat, filling the sails on the left-hand side.

Protractor. A simple instrument marked off in degrees, used to plot a course.

Reach. All points of sailing between running and sailing close-hauled.

Reef. To shorten the amount of sail exposed to the wind.

Reef knot. A square knot. See photograph, page 85.

Reef point. In some rigs, a light line running through a reef band on a sail, used for reefing.

Rig or rigging. Mast, boom, stays, shrouds, halyards, sheets, sails, and associated gear.

Rig. As a verb, this means to step the mast and secure the stays and shrouds.

Round turn. A second turn, or loop, around a ring or cleat or through a hole.

Rudder. A flat, movable piece attached upright to a boat's stern that can be turned, thus directing the boat's bow in one heading or another.

Running. A point of sailing on which a boat is sailing downwind, or with the wind.

Running rigging. Lines for raising and trimming the sails.

Shackle. A link.

Shackle. As a verb, to secure a shackle someplace.

Sheets. Lines which are used to control the sails.

Shoal waters. Shallow waters. Shoaling waters become ever shallower.

Shooting. Pointing into the wind while under way and coasting up to an object in the water.

Shrouds. Wires leading from the masthead to the sides of a boat which help support the mast.

Skeg. A triangular vertical projection on the bottom of a boat in the stern which helps direct the flow of water to the rudder.

Slab reefing. A simple, fast system of reefing in which the luff of a mainsail is hooked into a place on the boom and the sail is pulled taut with light lines often led through the boom.

Sloop. A single-masted sailboat with a fore and aft rig.

Slot effect. The result of the flow of air between a mainsail and a jib.

Splicing. Joining ends of separate lines, by interweaving the strands.

Spreaders. More or less horizontal struts on a mast which are high above the deck and separate the shrouds from each other and the mast.

Squall. A sudden gust of wind, often inconsiderable, but when associated with a squall line can bring strong and dangerous winds.

Standing rigging. Stays and shrouds, wires that hold a mast in place.

Starboard jibe. Running with the sails and boom on the port side.

Starboard side. Right-hand side.

Stays. Wires leading from the masthead to the bow, and to the stern, called respectively forestay and backstay.

Step. To put a mast in place.

Stern. The back end of a boat.

Stops. Narrow bands of cloth, lengths of rope or shock cord used to hold a sail in place.

Tack. The lower forward corner of a sail.

Tack. As a verb, proceeding to windward by sailing on alternate courses, with the wind first on one side, then the other. Also, to swing the bow of a boat from one tack to another, filling the sails on the opposite side.

Telltales. Wind indicators on your boat, strips of plastic, lengths of yarn.

Tidal currents. Currents caused by the ebb and flood of tides, as opposed to river currents.

Tiller. A bar connected to the head of a rudder, which is used to steer a boat.

Topsides. The sides of a boat above the water.

Transom. The stern facing of the hull of a boat.

True north. A geographic point marked on globes and maps. This seldom coincides with magnetic north.

True wind. The direction from which the wind is blowing. See the definition for apparent wind.

Turning turtle. Rolling over all the way so the mast is pointing downward.

Two half-hitches. A knot with uses similar to a clove hitch but less likely to become untied or slip. See photographic diagrams, page 86.

Vang. See boom vang.

Variation. The difference, in degrees, between true north and magnetic north in the region where you sail.

Wake. The path of turbulence which is created by a boat under way.

Waterline. A line indicating where the surface of the water ought to be when a boat is on an even keel, which helps suggest proper hull trim.

Way. Forward motion.

Whipping. Binding the end of a rope with a cord, so the rope will not unravel.

Winch. A spool-like mechanism used for bringing in, or winching, a sheet or anchor rode or raising and tightening a halyard. Blue Jays and similar small boats seldom are equipped with winches. Slightly larger boats often are, and big sailboats always carry winches.

Windward. When you point toward the wind, you are pointing to windward. Any object in the direction in which you are pointing is to windward of you.

Wing the jib. When running, to prop a jib out on a pole so that it fills on the side opposite from the mainsail.

Working jib. A jib that does not overlap the mainsail. A working jib is smaller than a Genoa jib. A storm jib is even smaller.

Charts and Tide and Current Tables

Parts of charts which are reproduced in this book should not be used for navigation. They are incomplete and out of date.

As this book goes to press, most United States charts are prepared by the National Ocean Survey of the National Oceanic and Atmospheric Administration, Department of Commerce. If you are an inland river sailor, you will probably need charts prepared by the U.S. Army Corps of Engineers. Canadian sailors will use charts prepared by Canada's Hydrographic Service.

In almost any populated place where people sail, you can buy the charts you need from stores selling boats and equipment used in boats. These stores sell tide and current tables, also published by the U.S. government and by Canada's Hydrographic Service.

Seek out local publications in addition to ones published by the U.S. and foreign governments. For example, *Eldridge Tide and Pilot Book,* often called Eldridge's, which is published every year, supplies the small-boat sailor with all kinds of information and includes tide and current tables for a variety of places from Nova Scotia to Key West and current tables for some places where the currents must be heeded.

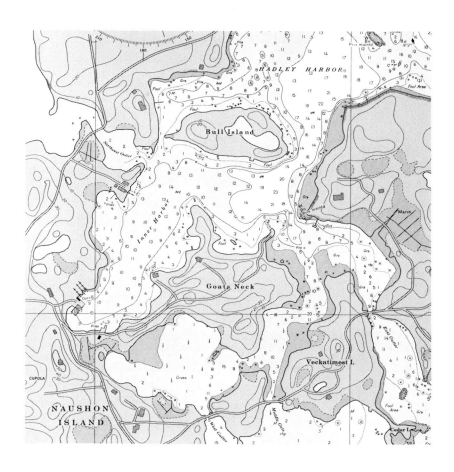

$\mathcal{O}$Index